101
COMMON THERAPEUTIC
BLUNDERS

101
COMMON THERAPEUTIC
BLUNDERS

Countertransference and
Counterresistance in Psychotherapy

Richard C. Robertiello, M.D.

and

Gerald Schoenewolf, Ph.D.

JASON ARONSON INC.
Northvale, New Jersey
London

10 9 8 7 6 5 4 3 2 1

Library of Congress Cataloging-in-Publication Data

Robertiello, Richard C.
  101 common therapeutic blunders.

  1. Countertransference (Psychology)—Case studies.
2. Psychotherapist and patient—Case studies.
3. Psychotherapy—Case studies. I. Schoenewolf,
Gerald. II. Title. III. Title: One hundred one common
therapeutic blunders. IV. Title: One hundred and one
common therapeutic blunders. [DNLM: 1. Countertransference (Psychology) 2. Physician-Patient Relations.
3. Psychotherapy. WM 62 R642z]
RC489.C68R63 1987   616.89'14   87-1406
ISBN 0-87668-960-8

Manufactured in the United States of America.

Contents

**7. Diagnosis and Treatment of Countertransference
and Counterresistance**
Richard C. Robertiello, M.D.

Preface

In the beginning there was the analysis of transference. Then there was the analysis of resistance. Now, more and more, there is also the analysis of countertransference and counterresistance. There has been an increasing recognition within the psychotherapy community that the therapist as well as the patient brings to the therapeutic relationship transferences and resistances that impede therapeutic progress. In fact, virtually every error a psychotherapist is likely to make is traceable to its countertransference and counterresistance roots.

This book presents 101 case histories of common pitfalls in psychotherapy. It is divided into two parts. The first comprises illustrative case histories of therapists' blunders stemming from erotic, sadomasochistic, and narcissistic countertransferences. The case histories in the second section portray two kinds of counterresistances – characterological (due to castration fear, narcissism, depression, etc.) and cultural (due to ethnic biases, belief systems, social values, etc.). The final chapter discusses ways therapists can diagnose and analyze themselves, and how they can best use supervision and therapy to resolve or prevent their blind spots and irrational behavior. It points out that the therapists' "occupational disease" is the very one they strive to "cure" in others.

Written primarily for professionals, this volume provides a practical "how-not-to" sourcebook rather than a theoretical treatise. The 101 case histories are intended as teaching tales in the

manner, say, of Sufi stories or *Aesop's Fables*. Hence, the volume
can be useful to therapists of all persuasions, including those not
using psychoanalytic techniques.

Acknowledgments

The case histories presented in this book, while based on actual
cases, have been fictionalized to preserve anonymity and to illustrate points more dramatically. Most were based on the authors'
own clinical experiences or on the work of therapists under their
direct supervision. A few were based on ideas suggested by the
writings of Heinrich Racker, Harold Searles, Hyman Spotnitz,
Ralph Greenson, and Frieda Fromm-Reichmann. We wish to express our gratitude to all involved – therapists and patients – in
these case histories, as well as to Lucy B. Smith, C.S.W., and
Jason Aronson, M.D., for their editorial advice and support.

CHAPTER ONE

COUNTERTRANSFERENCE AND COUNTERRESISTANCE

Gerald Schoenewolf, Ph.D.

When we think of transference and resistance we usually think of therapy patients. However, it has been pointed out by Freud and others that these processes can occur in or outside of the clinic. Many—if not most—people are caught up in the throes of transference and resistance, acting out a ritual of unreal behavior. They compulsively and impulsively live lives driven by unconscious forces and behave in ways that are destructive to themselves and others.

Therapists are not excepted from acting out transference and resistance feelings. When it occurs in the clinic, we call it countertransference and counterresistance. The problem is that patients come to us in order to get help in resolving their transference and resistance behavior, and when we respond with our own unresolved transference and resistance behavior, our ability to help them is greatly diminished. Our mission, so to speak, is to serve as models of realness.

We use the terms *countertransference* and *counterresistance* to represent all instances in which therapists act out feelings toward patients that are unresolved characerological or cultural conflicts or biases within themselves, whether or not induced by corresponding feelings in the patient. Our usage is an at-

tempt to transcend the varying current definitions of countertransference and counterresistance. We recognize that there are
clinical thinkers who subdivide countertransference into two categories: objective countertransference, which is induced by the
patient and which the therapist feels, without the temptation to
act out on it; and subjective countertransference, which represents an irrational response to the patient rooted in the therapist's fixations. Others subdivide counterresistance in the same
way. We think these are valid and useful categorizations.

Only in the first two or three years of a therapist's practice
are errors usually technical and not primarily a result of countertransference and counterresistance. During this period therapists are trying to apply the theories acquired during their formal
training. The most common technical errors have to do with
learning how to select interventions that work best with the
various patient types, making proper diagnostic formulations, ex-
tracting latent from manifest content, and maintaining therapeutic attitudes and boundaries that create an optimum environment
for each patient's particular needs. For example, there are
times—particularly in the beginning phase of treatment—when
therapists set up a holding environment in which trust can be
built; this is of particular importance for narcissistic patients. At
other times—especially during the middle phase—a more active,
confrontational stance may be required. These and similar technical procedures can usually be mastered early in the therapist's
career. Eventually, the focus of supervision shifts almost exclusively to issues of countertransference and counterresistance.

Unfortunately, when countertransference and counterresistance are operating, the therapist is at first not likely to be
aware of them, since they are linked to unconscious drives. A
major clue for the therapist is the rather intense feelings—either
erotic or aggressive—that are experienced at such times. A therapist "possessed" by countertransference feelings may find himself irresistably attracted to a patient, have murderous feelings,
or feel inordinately protective. When in the throes of counter-

resistance, therapists may find themselves reluctant to discuss certain subjects or unreceptive to certain kinds of feelings expressed by the patient, such as sexual or angry or loving feelings. Therapists under the sway of counterresistance may be silent, try to change the subject, or attempt to use interpretations to thwart a resisted idea or feeling. For example, a patient may express anger at the therapist who is resistant to anger; such a therapist may be hasty in interpreting that this anger does not belong to the therapist, but should be directed at the patient's parents. In cutting the patient off with this interpretation, the therapist does not give the patient the chance to ventilate feelings with the therapist in order to find out where the feelings belong, nor does the therapist in this situation give the patient the chance to discern the difference between the real relationship with the therapist and the transference relationship. Again, all of this is usually unconscious, and the therapist might employ rationalizations to justify such behavior. Only when a therapist pays close attention to the intense feelings aroused by a particular patient can there be awareness of the countertransference and counterresistance factors involved.

Even when therapists are conscious of experiencing countertransference or counterresistance feelings, they may attempt to deny them. Some therapists do not think they have the right to feel such emotions (particularly sexual or aggressive emotions); others are afraid of being swept away by them. In such cases, therapists are likely to defend themselves against the feelings by hiding behind their "therapeutic neutrality," offering inappropriate interventions in order to immediately push away the feelings, or expressing the feelings indulgently without regard for the patient's welfare. In any case, the therapist's reluctance to experience these feelings in an analytically appropriate manner then serves to reinforce the patient's already strong resistance to accepting and verbalizing his own transference feelings.

On the other hand, when utilized properly, countertransference and counterresistance feelings and urges can be a well of information from which to draw. The therapist who can tolerate the feelings being induced by the patient, who can clearly identify them, analyze them, and control them, has at his disposal, as Donald Winnicott points out, a "hands-on" experience of his love and hate in reaction to the actual personality and behavior of the patient, based on objective observation. When a therapist is on top of his countertransference and counterresistance feelings, he is running, rather than being run by, the therapy. He can use such feelings to creatively plan his working relationship with the patient in such a way as to ensure the most advantageous kind of outcome.

About Countertransference

Although much has been written about transference in the literature of psychoanalysis and psychotherapy, very little has been written about countertransference. Perhaps this is due to a narcissistic need of the psychotherapy community to view itself as "healthy" and patients as "unhealthy." Fortunately the situation has changed, with many contemporary publications, seminars, and conferences now devoted to this subject.

Sigmund Freud, in a letter to Sandor Ferenczi in 1910, introduced countertransference as an issue in therapy. Among the early contributors to the understanding of countertransference were Annie Reich, Maxwell Gitelson, and Ralph Greenson. Annie Reich made a distinction between general countertransference and countertransference proper (akin to the difference between objective and subjective countertransference) and was one of the first to note the problem of therapists acting out feelings toward patients. Maxwell Gitelson suggested abolishing the term *countertransference* and calling it instead "the analyst's transference to the patient." In his mind there was no difference between the patient's transference and the analyst's transference – a view which today is widely held. Ralph Greenson stressed the importance of the therapist's real relationship with the patient as contrasted with the transference/countertransference relationship—a point with which we concur.

Heinrich Racker in *Transference and Countertransference* introduced the concept of countertransference neurosis, defining it as an independent entity, the pathological part of the countertransference and the expression of neurosis. In the countertransference neurosis (subjective countertransference), formerly repressed feelings are released, just as in the transference neurosis—except it is the therapist who releases irrational feelings at the expense of the patient. Both Racker and Reich assert the universality of this phenomenon and point out that, if they wish to function maximally in the analytic situation, therapists must be aware of their transferences to the patient and neutralize them; if they are unaware of them, they are likely to act them out in order to (1) live out the underlying, often infantile id impulses; (2) defend against these id impulses; and (3) prove that no damage has occurred in consequence of these impulses.

A gifted psychoanalyst, Racker was the first to thoroughly explore the patient/therapist relationship as a two-sided one in which both patient and therapist are required to resolve their transferences and overcome their resistances. Racker also was one of the first to note that countertransference feelings could be used by therapists as a gauge as to what was going on in the patient's unconscious. For example, if a therapist began to feel bored, he or she could surmise that the patient was avoiding something; if a therapist was feeling angry at a patient, that would usually indicate the patient wanted to make the therapist angry; and if a therapist began to feel sexually aroused, that was attributed as having been induced by a patient's unconscious seductiveness. The countertransference, then, was seen by Racker as just as important in the treatment as the transference.

The transference, according to Freud, is the field in which the principal battles are fought by the patient and the therapist, in order to conquer the patient's resistances. Racker believed that the countertransference is the other half of this field, on which the principal battles are fought to conquer the analyst's resistances, that is, the counterresistances.

At the beginning of the therapy relationship almost nothing real goes on between therapist and patient. The patient defends against long-repressed feelings that might become activated within the context of this new relationship, and the therapist slowly attempts to interpret to the patient how he is resisting being real. The transference/countertransference relationship marks the beginning of a process that will lead to an authentic relationship between the human being who is the patient and the human being who is the therapist. However, at first it is a relationship rooted in the past. The patient and the therapist are primarily symbolic objects to each other, and virtually everything that is said and done in their present relationship is a reactivation of attitudes and situations which applied to figures, usually parents or siblings, from the past. It is the therapist's task to help the patient become authentic again, by guiding him toward being real with the therapist.

Racker compares the basic principle of analytic technique to the ancient Socratic injunction to "know thyself." He sees analysis as helping the patient achieve union with himself through a full conscious and emotional acceptance of everything that was once pathologically disowned during early childhood. This union with oneself implies overcoming the anxiety and fear of one's disowned self and the means which one uses to defend against this anxiety and fear. Racker lists such defense mechanisms as splitting, mutilation, denial, annihilation, closing-up (deadening oneself), projecting oneself onto the world and then quarreling with it in order to alleviate internal discord, and withdrawing from the world to maintain a semblance of inner peace. The analytic technique attempts to bring back one's real self, to reunite with what was lost on the way to adulthood.

In the therapeutic relationship, the attention of the therapist is focused on the return of all the infantile processes that have been repressed (that is, on the emergence of the patient's unconscious). It is in and through this return, the transference, that the therapist attempts to overcome the patient's destructive methods of defending himself or herself. By linking what happens in the patient's relationship with the external world with what happens in the transference to the therapist, the therapist can put it all together and, using his countertransference feelings, tell the patient what the patient needs to know in order to permit the union of conscious and unconscious selves.

Therapists must therefore remain steadfast and empathic in the face of their patients' transferred hostility toward them, their sexual acting out, and any other provocative and normally inflammatory situations. To be a therapist requires one not to retaliate, not to enter into the neurotic vicious circle, not to submit to the patient's defensive maneuvers or be sucked into his or her attempts to sabotage the relationship, but to be continually searching for understanding and battling against the patient's transference as well as one's own countertransference. To help a patient be authentic again, the therapist must be authentic. The therapist must ultimately spend as much time analyzing his own transference as he does the patient's.

In addition, the therapist must know how to use countertransference. More recently, analysts such as Robert Langs, Harold Searles, Hyman Spotnitz, and D. W. Winnicott have addressed this problem. Langs points out how therapists induce transferences, often unwittingly, and provides a detailed framework for controlling the therapist–patient forcefield. Searles, Spotnitz, and Winnicott demonstrate how therapists may express countertransference feelings to break an impasse, to show the patient what impact he or she is having on the therapist, or to immunize the patient to aggression (the patient's or the therapist's). They contend that therapists who are in tune with themselves need not hide behind a blank screen.

About Counterresistance

Racker defined the analyst's counterresistances as coinciding with resistances in the patient that concern the same situation. It is as though there is a tacit agreement between therapist and patient to keep quiet on a certain topic. A patient may convey a resistance to hearing interpretations. A therapist, who has difficulty with this same issue, develops a counterresistance to interpreting. The therapy may stay at a virtual standstill. Racker saw counterresistances mainly as the expression of the therapist's identification with the patient's resistances (which at the same time might also be related to a conflict in the therapist's past). We agree, up to a point; however, there are situations in which the counterresistance stems almost exclusively from the therapist, and we have included several cases to illustrate this point.

Other analysts have pointed out that in actuality resistance is an aspect of transference. The patient's transference to the therapist—so this point of view goes—acts as a resistance to his or her feelings in general and to specific infantile material. The negative transference can be an attempt to ward off (resist) deeper, infantile feelings of longing and oedipal feelings of sexual attraction toward the therapist; the patient unconsciously anticipates that the therapist (like the transferred parents) will reject, exploit, or abuse these feelings. The positive transference (falling in love with, admiring, desiring the therapist) can likewise be a resistance to feelings of infantile rage and hostility; the patient fears his or her rage will destroy the therapeutic relationship, antagonize the therapist, and bring about a retaliation.

Psychoanalysts who have written thusly about counterresistance have considered it, likewise, to be part of the countertransference. The therapist reacts to the patient's negative transference with a negative countertransference, or to the patient's positive transference with a positive countertransference. In either case, the therapist will then be counterresistant to the same infantile feelings within himself against which the patient is defending, and counterresistant to analyzing his or her own feelings towards the patient, as well as the patient's feelings. In this book, we will call all resistances that stem from countertransference reactions characterological counterresistances.

Hyman Spotnitz, founder of "modern psychoanalysis," who first used the terms *subjective* and *objective* in categorizing types of countertransference, has also devised useful terms to designate types of characterological resistances by patients. He has labeled as "treatment-destructive resistances" those forms of behavior that, particularly during the beginning phase of treatment, attempt to sabotage and destroy the therapeutic relationship. Such behaviors include coming late, missing appointments, forgetting to pay, coming to sessions drunk or under the influence of other drugs, opposing virtually everything the therapist suggests, and showing unbridled hostility or seductiveness. "Status quo resistances" refer to more subtle forms of behavior, usually occurring during the middle phase of treatment, that are aimed at preventing any change in the relationship.

Although Spotnitz does not do so, we believe these terms can also be applied to counterresistance; therapists are also guilty of treatment-destructive resistances at times, and they are even more prone to status quo resistances. Treatment-destructive resistances by therapists include missing appointments, falling asleep during sessions, drinking or taking other drugs during sessions, and severely overcharging patients. Status quo resistances by therapists, like those by patients, involve subtle forms of behavior designed to resist any change in the relationship and to cling to the safety and security of the status quo, although the status quo may be in reality a nonrelationship. A therapist who resists hearing a patient's negative feelings about the therapy situation is acting out such a resistance.

We can expand the definition of resistance and counterresistance to include influences that fall outside the realm of transference and countertransference, positing the term *cultural counterresistances*. For example, a liberal-minded therapist who is resistant to hearing a conservative patient's opinions about social issues and hence falls silent, changes the subject, or in other ways expresses a judgment about those views is, we believe, acting out a counterresistance that is not an aspect of the countertransference per se but, rather, an expression of values rooted in the cultural milieu in which the therapist was brought up. Thus, in this book we put great emphasis on internalized societal values, fixed belief systems, biases, and the like. The therapist not only has to help the patient overcome his or her biases, belief systems, and values insofar as they serve as resistances, but also must overcome his or her own cultural counterresistances.

We recognize that a case might be made that societal values, fixed belief systems, biases, and the like are also aspects of neurosis, and as such may also be seen as characterological defenses. But, again, for simplicity's sake we have made the distinction between characterological and cultural counterresistances, convinced that such a distinction is an aid to our understanding of the wellsprings of counterresistance.

Resistance, like transference, is present to some degree in all relationships—not just in therapy. In fact, to not resist would mean to be completely vulnerable, completely open, both to our own primitive feelings and urges and to those of others (as we are in early childhood before resistances set in); this is not the aim of therapy. If we let go of resistances (defenses) entirely and all at once, we become susceptible to "the thousand and one shocks the flesh is heir to." The aim of therapy is to allow people to let go of resistances gradually—for example, in their relationships with lovers or friends or with their own creativity. For it is our loving, spontaneous, creative experiences in life that make living worthwhile. To participate fully in these events is what gives life meaning and makes it a pleasure rather than a struggle. Therapists who have not reached the point at which they can truly let go of their resistances when the situation calls for it, either in their personal lives or in their therapy relationships, are preventing both themselves and their patients from growing.

The concept of counterresistance is still somewhat controversial in the more traditional schools of psychoanalysis; by devoting an entire section of this book to the subject, we are trying to make a statement in defense of the concept as well as bring it on a par with the concept of resistance, where it rightfully belongs.

Most people spend their lives transferring and resisting. Freud wrote about the unconscious, where humankind hides its deeper motives from itself, and Jung referred to the collective unconscious, which serves the same purpose for humankind as a mass. Winnicott wrote about the false self and the real self, and Eric Berne pointed out the "games people play."

To transfer and resist is to be false, to be unable to look at oneself objectively, to be unconscious, and to play games, all of which precludes being real, emotionally involved, actualized, humane, and wise. We hope the following 101 case histories will serve not only as a practical reference source, but also as a reminder of our own professional fallibility.

PART ONE

SIXTY-ONE
COUNTERTRANSFERENCE
BLUNDERS

Introduction

These case histories demonstrate a variety of countertransference dilemmas faced by psychoanalysts and psychotherapists. They were chosen because of their universality and clarity. Further, they have been written to convey not only the interpsychic and intrapsychic issues, but also the human aspects of the patient–therapist dyad. We want the reader not only to grasp intellectually the dynamics of the situation, but also to get a feel for those dynamics. Hence, the style of presentation is a bit more literary than is usual for professional works.

The case histories have been arranged under three categories—erotic, sadomasochistic, and narcissistic—because these cover all the characterologically rooted countertransference blunders that therapists are likely to make. There will be some overlapping, for in most cases subjective countertransference represents a mixture of unresolved oral, anal, and oedipal derivatives. For example, a therapist may have a desire to control a patient that is partly a sadomasochistic and partly a narcissistic countertransference (an acting out of dominance needs or grandiosity).

Erotic countertransference feelings may be the most difficult of all for a therapist to be aware of, manage, and utilize. Even though we have undergone a sexual revolution in recent years and the subject of sexuality is not the taboo it once was, it is still an issue fraught with controversy. If analysts themselves cannot discuss this issue, how are they to deal effectively with erotic countertransference in the therapeutic situation!

And these feelings do come up in therapy again and again. It is quite common for patients of both sexes to be seductive toward their therapists. Being seductive is both a way of pleasing a therapist (showing sexual interest) and an attempt to wrest control from the therapist, bringing the therapist down from the perch of professionalism. Therapists who have not resolved their sexual or narcissistic needs may find themselves tempted to act out these needs. In addition, therapists may fail to understand or empathize with patients because of their own unresolved erotic conflicts. For example, a patient may tell a therapist who has just experienced an unhappy love relationship, and whose relationship with his mother was also unhappy, about problems of a similar nature with his current lover and mother. This therapist may then become overinvolved in helping this patient. Or, suppose a female therapist who has unresolved feelings of penis envy works with a male patient who had a castrating mother and needs to affirm his manhood. Will the therapist unwittingly behave as to reinforce the patient's low self-esteem? Or, a patient relates the details of her sexual relationship; will the patient's therapist (male or female) vicariously live through the patient, using this explicit sexual material, perhaps even encouraging it, in order to fill a void in his or her own life? Will this reaction prevent the therapist from properly listening to, empathizing with, and analyzing the patient's transference and resistance?

With sadomasochistic countertransferences, the danger is always that the therapist will become involved in a power struggle with the patient. Sometimes the therapist has a need to dominate, manipulate, or control the patient (act sadistically), in which case the therapist may view the patient as a wild beast who needs taming. Or the therapist may have an unconscious need to be dominated, controlled, or manipulated by the patient (act masochistically), in which case the therapist will view the patient as a persecutor.

A sadomasochistic therapist may, for instance, use the patient as a vehicle for proving his own skills and powers as a therapist. Such therapists may conduct the treatment in a way that disregards their patients' real needs and desires. Other therapists may insist that their patients accept their interpretations without question, as though they were the law, and become irritated when their patients do not accept them as such. Patients in these instances will feel they are being used to satisfy the therapist's need for power and will respond with an attitude of defiance or compliance; in each case nothing real will happen. Some therapists force patients to do and accomplish things—lying on the couch, free associating, performing a gestalt exercise—before they are ready, and the patient is again put in the position of either complying or defying. Eventually the therapy will fail.

A patient's hostility will often elicit a sadomasochistic countertransference reaction. It is a given that at some point in successful therapy all patients express hostility to their therapists. Usually this hostility is expressed through criticism of their therapists, and those therapists who have not completely worked through their own feelings of anger at parental figures will be unable to tolerate their patients' hostility. They may attempt to encourage patients to express hostility, thereby unwittingly causing patients to do just the opposite (why express hostility to a person who invites you to do so; defiance gets the job done so much more easily). Or they may attempt to analyze the hostility before it is completely vented, or may behave in such a warm and loving way as to preclude the expression of hostility. They may get into a power struggle with their patients, again viewing the patient as a beast who must be tamed (through sadistic interpretations) or as a persecutor who must be endured. In this case the therapist becomes martyr, attempting through a kind of thera-

peutic anal retention and passive aggression to bring the patient
to his knees.

Narcissistic countertransferences involve the acting out of
feelings of low self-esteem, rage, depression, or dependency. For
example, narcissistic therapists sometimes have a need to be always right, to be "perfect" therapists, because of their self-
esteem problems. As a result, they may put pressure on their patients to get well, which may cause them to deteriorate or
regress. Other therapists acting out narcissistic feelings will try
to impress patients; the patients will act duly impressed, and a
collusion will be formed: the therapist becomes the "good daddy"
and the patient the "good child," and hardly anything real will
happen. Again, therapists with narcissistic features may attempt
to bolster their insecurity by cultivating idealization and admiration. This will interfere with the therapists' ability to listen and
will keep the patient in a stage of dependence, instead of enhanc-
ing ego strengths and autonomy, growth, independence, and original judgment.

Sometimes narcissistic therapists have the attitude that
they are "gods" who are going to remold the patient in their own
image. They will then have an agenda for the patient that will invariably be in opposition to the patient's needs. The patient will
be expected to become a narcissistic extension, to accept the therapist's values and work out his or her personal problems the same
way the therapist did. A narcissistic therapist who is depressed
may call upon the patient, through unconscious nonverbal language, for protection or rescue. If the therapist is wounded
narcissistically by the patient—because the latter fails to rescue
the therapist or expresses hostility instead—the therapist may
react with narcissistic rage.

These are but a few of the countertransference situations
that arise. In the pages that follow we illustrate the most common
of these situations—ones that occur in all forms of psychotherapy.

CHAPTER TWO

EROTIC
COUNTERTRANSFERENCES

Blunder 1

The Therapist and the Chorus Girl

"I could always seduce just about anybody I wanted to," she told her therapist, a young male, during her first session. She continued in a matter-of-fact way to tell him about her compulsive pattern. "The trouble is, once I seduce them I lose interest. And also I'm always attracted to the wrong kind of men. I have this habit — it's embarrassing to tell you this — I have this habit of getting involved with married men. In fact, several of them left their wives for me. Then I have contempt for them. I can't stand them anymore."

For the next few sessions she elaborated on this pattern, while also filling him in on other details of her life. A beautiful woman with an innocent face and full, pouty lips and blue eyes, she had for many years made a living as a night club dancer. Now that she was 35 years old, she had entered a master's degree program in dance therapy, wanting to establish a career that did not rely on her looks. As an aside, she mentioned that she had been sexually abused as a child and that she had had affairs with both men and women.

Meanwhile, as she spoke about her pattern with men, her career problems, her childhood, something entirely different was happening on a nonverbal level. During the first and second sessions, for example, she had sat for several minutes at a time with her legs spread apart, revealing herself fully to the therapist (she always wore dresses to the sessions). And during the fourth session she stopped at one point and made quite a deal out of adjusting her bra, reaching inside her bodice with her right hand, fiddling for a minute, and exclaiming, "I think the snap is broken." Then, making a girlish, cross-eyed smirk, she proceeded with her discourse on men. "I think deep down all men are jerks," she was saying. "I haven't found one I can trust." And it happened that at that point she suddenly turned to the therapist and snapped, "What do you think about all this? Do you talk?"

"Yes, I talk," he replied, taken aback. "You sound angry."

"Well, you're not saying anything. You're just sitting there like a bump on a log. I'd like some feedback. That's why I came here."

"What kind of feedback would you like?"

"I don't know. Anything." She glowered at him with her pouty eyes.

The therapist, who had not been practicing very long and who was seeing this woman in connection with an internship at a low fee, found himself feeling a mixture of sexual excitement, anxiety, and anger. He was so flooded with feelings he could not sort them out and therefore did not know what to say.

The patient had induced a strong countertransference in him, as she had done with previous therapists; she had a history of going from therapist to therapist, never staying for more than a few sessions, always finding them lacking. She expected each therapist to be a hypocritical, exploitative, sexually abusive authority figure (as both her father and mother had been), and so she set it up that way with each therapist. In essence, she had put this therapist in a double bind: if he responded to her seductiveness, she would have contempt for him, and if he did not respond, she would be insulted.

On his part, the therapist had become immobilized by conflicting feelings. On one hand, he wanted to make love to her, and on the other hand he wanted to strangle her, or at least shake her. The patient had become, on an unconscious, countertransference plane, his teasing mother, who had often paraded her nude body in front of him when he was a child, and who, when he had made any attempt to reach out to her, would tell him he was a naughty boy. He wanted to do to this woman now what he had often fantasized about doing to his mother. Hence he was not able to be empathic, to hang in there and be the trusting, supportive father figure she was so desperately searching for. Instead, he counter-attacked.

"You really want feedback?" he finally spoke up. "Let me ask you something. Are you aware of how you're sitting?"

"What do you mean?" she replied with surprise.

"You're sitting with your legs spread out so I can see right up your dress." There was an edge of anger in his voice.

She looked down with horror. "Oh!" She quickly crossed her legs and adjusted the skirt, blushing. "I didn't realize it. I sit this way all the time when I'm wearing pants. I don't know what you're getting at."

"And a few minutes ago you made a great show of adjusting your bra."

"So?" There was anger in her voice, too. "What's your point?"

"The point is that I'm experiencing you as being seductive with *me* right now."

"Are you sure it's not just wishful thinking?"

The therapist, in an exasperated manner, attempted to interpret for her that she was attempting to seduce him as she did other unavailable men in her life, that the pattern was continuing right here before their very eyes. However, because he was angry and because he was unable to focus on her positive need to experience a trusting relationship with him, and because the timing of the interpretation was way off, she heard not a word of it.

At the end of the session she walked out in a huff. During the middle of the week she called to tell him she was quitting therapy and intended to look for a female therapist. He wished her luck, then added somewhat tentatively, "If you change your mind and you'd like to come in to discuss this, please feel free to do so."

"I won't," she replied, and hung up.

Blunder 2

The Therapist and the Virgin

When she first came to see her young male therapist, an attractive female told him she was a virgin. She was a Catholic and he was a Catholic; hence both had been raised in a cultural environment in which virginity was extolled. And so a collusion was formed; he became her father-confessor, and she became his pure daughter-madonna. Theirs was a very positive transference/countertransference relationship.

Then one day she confessed that she had not been honest with him. "Actually," she said, "I'm not a virgin. I've been having an affair since before I began therapy. I don't know why I was afraid to tell you that. I guess I thought I had to be a virgin for you."

She was right. The therapist reacted with anger to this confession and could not bring himself to even talk about it, much less analyze it. He fell silent for the remainder of the session and became increasingly cold toward her in the sessions that followed.

Her confession was experienced by the therapist as a betrayal, one that brought up feelings from early childhood, when he had first realized that his mother was not his alone but was having sex with his father. Up until that point the mother had been pure in his eyes; afterward he saw her as a witch. Similarly, now he saw his patient as a whore and a witch for having sexual relations and lying about it. He also felt narcissistically wounded, as though he had been fed bad milk.

As the result of this change in his attitude, the patient's attitude also changed. She deeply resented her therapist's silence and coldness, experiencing it as a rejection of her sexual feelings—a rejection that rekindled traumatic memories of being treated coldly by her father when she had gone through the oedipal stage and made romantic advances at him. To defend against the therapist's rejection, she began to act more and more seductive around him, out of spite (just as she had with her father). He interpreted this seductive behavior in an accusatory manner, citing it as a form of resistance.

"I was just being playful," she replied, feeling attacked by him. "You therapists never want to have fun."

Thereafter she herself fell into many silences that resembled the silences of the therapist, and they now got stuck in another collusion, a collusion of silences, an impasse of noncommunication that lasted for many months.

Blunder 3

The Therapist Who Gave Hugs

A young male patient went to his older, but still attractive, female therapist complaining that his previous therapist had refused to give him a hug.

"All I wanted was just one hug," he said in a sad, bitter tone of voice. He was a tall, blue-eyed, sensitive young man who might have passed for a choirboy. "She kept telling me it would spoil the therapeutic relationship if she hugged me, and I kept telling her that it would spoil it if she didn't; so now I'm here."

"What would it mean to you if I gave you a hug?" the therapist asked.

"Oh, God. Are you going to start that? That's what *she* always did. She was *always* pulling that psychoanalytic crap. Look, can't you just give me a hug? I don't want analysis right now. I want to be soothed. I didn't get enough soothing when I was a kid, okay? Just give me a little soothing, a little comfort, and then we'll do the analysis. After all, even such classical analysts as the Blancks recommend using parameters at times," he added, being versed in analytic literature.

The therapist could not help but be charmed by this precocious young man. At the end of the session she hugged him

good-by. She did likewise at the end of the next session and also at
the end of the one after that. The patient became outwardly compliant after that, appearing to plunge into analytic work, and the
hugs seemed to bring about therapeutic progress. Then, after
about the sixth hug, the young man drew away from the therapist
and gazed rapturously into her eyes. She in turn looked into his,
smiling shyly, taken by his soft blue eyes, his wholesome skin, his
pouty lips. They kissed. The therapist pulled away.

"We shouldn't be doing this."

"I know," the young man said. "But we are."

"But I'm your therapist. It's. . . ."

"You *were* my therapist."

What happened? Having given in to the first hug, the therapist had already lost this patient. He had succeeded in manipulating her into giving him a hug, and after that initial maneuver she
was under his sway. She became increasingly excited by his hugs
and was unable to turn down his advance because, in effect, he
had seduced her. This man had seduced the therapist by putting
her into a no-win situation. If she turned down his request for a
hug, he would leave her as he did his last therapist; if she gave in,
he would be in control of the therapy.

Consciously she thought she could handle the situation,
rationalizing that she would give him just one hug. Then she rationalized that since the therapy was going better she would continue giving him the hugs, choosing not to see the superficial nature of his compliance. On an unconscious level she was acting out
a narcissistic need for closeness with her mother, and an oedipal
need to rescue her father and take him away from her mother.
Her father had been an alcoholic, and, when the therapist had
been a little girl of 4 and 5 and 6, she had often witnessed her father's binges and her mother's castigation of her father. Often her
father had come to her for consolation, and she would sit in his lap
and hug him and tell him everything was going to be all right.
But, of course, everything was not all right, and as soon as the father had sobered up he would forget all about his daughter's min-

istrations. And if, when he was sober, the daughter came to him for a hug, he would rebuke her, saying, "I'm trying to read the paper. Do you mind?"

So these frustrated hugs and the desire to rescue and run away with her father, combined with the narcissistic need to merge again with a rejecting mother, got acted out on a counter-transferential level with this patient. Hence, the therapy was sabotaged.

Blunder 4

The Therapist Who Castrated Himself

A female patient was referred to a therapist by his supervisor (his father-surrogate), whose opinion with regard to his capacity as an analyst was very important to him. The patient, a young woman prone to physical ailments, manifested a great deal of anxiety stemming from unresolved oral and erotic needs. The therapist tried to "feed" her for several months without success. Then he himself began feeling anxious and became ill.

The idea had occurred to the therapist that if the treatment failed, he would be violently criticized and persecuted by the supervisor. His superego was projected upon this real object; the danger he felt threatened by was castration – since to practice the profession meant, on the oedipal level, to castrate the father and conquer the mother. In defense against this situation – that is to say, where the ego is defending itself against persecution by a very severe superego – a psychosomatic response may arise. The cruel superego is not only the father who threatens to castrate, but also the devouring mother of preoedipal times: the poisonous breast.

In this instance, the therapist was literally making himself sick, that is, "castrating" himself in order to appease his archaic persecuting superego (the castrating father-supervisor). Then, as the patient began to feel better and he himself was feeling worse, he began to hate the patient, blaming her "vampirism" for his own illness. However, it was not her vampirism that did him in, but his own countertransference, due to oedipal and preoedipal conflicts that were aroused by the circumstances of her therapy with him. In effect, he took on her illness and she got better, but without really resolving the underlying psychic conflicts.

In discussing the situation with his supervisor, he was able to understand and come to grips with his countertransference feelings. The supervisor made it clear to the therapist that the therapist was making the supervisor into his father-surrogate. "I'm not here to judge you. I'm here to help you," the supervisor told him. They analyzed the entire situation, and the therapist went away feeling quite relieved. Within a few weeks his health had improved, and he was able to interpret to the patient the dynamics of the situation between them, putting the relationship back on track.

Blunder 5

The Therapist
Who Had Not Resolved Her Penis Envy

A young man had seen a female therapist for about a year. He had noticed that every time he talked about his sexual feelings toward women, his therapist would either fall into a deep silence or quickly divert the conversation away from the subject of sex. This young man had a castrating mother, one who had continually put down his masculinity in various ways. For instance, when he was an adolescent and he asked his mother to pick up a pair of jockey shorts, she laughed at him and said, "What do you need a pair of jockey shorts for?" Because the man had been emasculated in this way by his mother, he had a need to brag about his penis, about how big it was, and about his exploits with women. On her part, the female therapist could not handle this boasting. Whenever he began to talk in this way, she felt revulsion and anger and could scarcely restrain the impulse to tell him he was a male chauvinist jerk and that he should get out of her office immediately. Because she had not resolved her penis envy and the associated anger and contempt toward men, she could not handle this man's sexual boasting; so she lapsed into a deep silence or changed the subject.

The young man sensed, of course, that the woman was uncomfortable with his discussions of his sexual adventures, and he felt this as a sexual rejection, which made him want to talk about his sexuality and brag even more. Deep down, on a transferential level, he was seeking the sexual affirmation he never got from his mother.

One day, after failing to get a response from her for over a year, the man was driven to try a new tack.

"You know," he said to her. "I don't think you really believe that I'm good in bed. I get the impression you think I'm a braggart."

"What makes you think that?" she replied somewhat anxiously.

"I don't know. Something in your manner."

"Oh, really." The therapist felt too anxious to ask him what he saw in her manner.

"I was thinking. . . ." He looked at her, a small smile on his face.

"Yes?"

"I was thinking maybe I ought to demonstrate it to you."

"What do you mean?"

"I was thinking I'd like to fuck you."

He smiled at her. It was a seductive, aggressive smile, for he was very angry at her by that time, having felt rejected and castrated by her, which had, in turn, rekindled the feelings of rage at his mother.

The therapist was mortified. At first she glared at him, stunned. She was both terrified and angry. Her countertransference made it impossible for her to understand him and empathize with his need for affirmation. Instead she saw him as a "conceited prick" like her father, whom she had always felt rejected by and whom she still resented. She was furious at him.

"No," she finally replied. "I don't think that would be a good idea." There was an obvious tone of contempt in her voice.

"Why not?" he persisted, the smile still on his face. He had been driven to the point where, unconsciously, he wanted to shock her, wanted to force her to see him as a man, to respond to his masculinity.

"I just don't think it would be a good idea, that's all."

"I could fuck you like you've never been fucked before."

"I'm sure you could, but that's not the point." The therapist seemed to flinch a bit, eyeing the patient crossly. At that moment she found herself getting excited, having a fantasy of being taken by the patient; she was at the same time angry at herself for having these feelings and angry at the patient for eliciting them. "That's really not the point at all," she added.

"I could fuck your brains out," he said.

"I really don't want to continue with this subject."

"Why not?"

"I don't think it's productive."

"You don't think it's productive," he said, mimicking her. "Fuck you. *I* think it's productive."

"Look," she said, standing up suddenly, hugging herself. "I don't think this is working. I think you'd better leave."

"You want me to leave?"

"That's right."

"But why? You said I could say anything I wanted to in here."

"I know. I'm sorry. I'd like you to leave. I think maybe you need a male therapist. I'm sorry, I just don't think it's working." She was trembling with rage. "Would you please leave?"

The patient was also in a rage. He had gone to the therapist in order to resolve his castration fear and reaffirm his masculinity, but had instead met a therapist who was, unconsciously, just as castrating as his mother. The therapist was unconsciously castrating, primarily because of unresolved sibling rivalry and penis envy. When this woman was 3 years old and had discovered for the first time the pleasure of masturbation, her mother scolded her, saying, "That's dirty. Don't do that." However, she noticed that her brother, who was a year older than she, often played with his penis and was never scolded by her mother. Still later, when she asked her mother why she didn't have a penis, her mother again scolded her, saying, "Don't ask such silly questions." Naturally the girl had to repress her feelings about these matters, including a lot of jealousy and hatred of her brother. These later came to the surface with respect to the young man who now boasted to her about his sexuality. Because she had been in a training analysis with an analyst who did not believe in penis envy, the therapist had never resolved these issues.

The result was that she lost this patient and, in addition, drove him to an even greater rage than he had possessed when he came to her. A better response on her part would have been to listen empathically to the young man's boasting and be supportive in a way that his mother had not been, until such time as he had acquired the sufficient ego strength to give up such posturing and see it for the compensatory defensive position that it was. Had it not been for her countertransference, she might have been able to do that.

Blunder 6

The Homophobic Therapist

A young therapist was treating a man in his middle thirties – a sensitive, highly intelligent, physically handsome man – with whom he had much in common. For many months the therapist endured fits of sarcasm, name calling, and other forms of rejecting behavior as he helped the patient work through his negative transference. The patient had had a similar relationship with his mother, one in which sarcasm and name calling were prevalent, and now it was repeated in the therapy relationship. The therapist had no problems handling this transference. However, when the negative transference was resolved and the patient began one day to speak of his love for, and sexual attraction toward, the therapist, the latter found himself feeling anxious. At that time he had not yet worked through those feelings in his personal analysis.

At this point in the therapy the patient was offered a job in another city. The therapist, rather than seeing the patient's sudden desire to move away as a resistance, found many reasons why it would be best for the patient to do just that. "You seem to be doing much better now," the therapist told the patient. "I think this move makes a lot of sense." The patient accepted the new position and terminated therapy a month later.

Blunder 7

The Good Daddy

There was a certain elderly male therapist who was known to be sweet, kind, gentle, and generous in spirit and in deed. He was beloved by all of his patients, most of whom were young women, and hardly any of them ever left him. For each of his patients, he would play the role of the good daddy—the wise, responsive, understanding, older man to whom these young women could turn with problems concerning their boyfriends or husbands. In essence, he would have a little romance with each patient, and the romance would literally never end, going on for years and years. Often, when a patient was feeling distraught, he would have her sit on his lap and would comfort her, and usually when she left he would see her to the door and peck her on the cheek or forehead or sometimes even on the lips.

Yes, he had learned about erotic transferences during his training, and he knew that such transferences should be analyzed, in order to resolve the complexes and narcissistic fixations and other repressed conflicts that lay beneath, yet somehow he could not bring himself to do so. He told himself he did not want to hurt his patients' feelings. In truth he was acting out his own oedipal and narcissistic feelings. As a child he had learned quickly what his mother wanted from him. She called him "my little friend," and she would hug him very tightly after she had had a fight with his father, and the boy felt good to be able to give his mother comfort.

Now he felt equally good to be able to give his young female patients comfort. And so both he and his patients lived happily ever after in a state of mutual dependency, living out a permanently unrequited love relationship. And consequently little analysis or resolution of deep conflicts occurred.

Blunder 8

The Therapist Who Fell in Love

On her third session an attractive young woman brought her middle-aged therapist a bouquet of daisies, saying, "I just wanted you to have these because I think you're so nice." The therapist, who was recently divorced and lonely, thanked her for the flowers and had a momentary fantasy of taking her into his arms and kissing her. The fantasy passed.

On her sixth session she brought him a coffee mug, having noticed that the one he had been using until then was cracked. Again he thanked her, and again he had a sexual fantasy.

After several months of this, the young woman came to him one day and exclaimed, "I think I'm in love with you."

"That's nice," the therapist said, feeling anxious.

Then she proceeded to tell him a dream. She had dreamed the night before that she was at the therapist's office, she was in love with him and he was in love with her, they embraced, and both were joyously happy. She beamed and blushed as she told him the dream.

The therapist, feeling even more anxious, attempted to follow standard analytic procedure. "What would it mean to you if I were in love with you and you with me?" he asked.

"I guess it would mean that you appreciated me the same way I appreciate you."

"And how do you appreciate me?"

"I think you're the most wonderful man I've ever met."

The therapist was taken aback by the young woman's unabashed directness. "But you don't really know me."

"I know what I feel."

"Well," the therapist recovered. "All right. Then I suppose you'd like me to think you're the most wonderful woman I've ever met?"

She shrugged her shoulders in a childlike way. "I guess so."

"And then what. What do we do if we're in love in this way?"

"I don't know. I guess we'd have to stop doing therapy and have a regular relationship."

"I see. And what about your problems. What about your agoraphobia and your bad relationships with men that caused you to come to me in the first place?"

"I don't know. . . ." She gazed directly into the therapist's eyes, and he sighed deeply to allay his anxiety.

During the week between this session and her next session he thought about this patient constantly. He had fantasies of making love to her, marrying her, having children with her, moving to far-off, exotic places with her. He looked forward to her next visit with a longing he could not understand. Then, upon her next session, she entered beaming and informed him that she had broken up with her boyfriend.

"I decided I like older men," she said, gazing into his eyes.

He attempted once again to analyze her transference toward him, but his heart wasn't really in it. There was a small smile at the edges of his lips as he attempted to probe her feelings about him, and there was also a small smile at the edges of her lips and in her eyes, and it was as if the two of them shared a secret. At the end of the session he stood and went to his desk to write something down. She strolled up behind him to give him his check. When he turned around she stood beaming in front of him. Abruptly he grabbed her, held her tightly for a moment, gazed in her eyes—which shone brightly now as a child's—and kissed her. Then she pulled away, the smile left her face, and she gawked at him in a curious way. Then she ran out of the room.

She called him during the week and told him on the phone that she had decided to quit therapy. She said she had talked to her boyfriend about it—they were back together again—and he had advised her to seek another therapist. She thought that would be best under the circumstances.

The therapist had obviously given in to his countertransference feelings and had consequently gotten stung. Because of his own unfulfilled needs for love and approval, due not only to his recent divorce but also to a depriving relationship with his mother, he lost sight of the fact that his patient's proclamations of love for him were an acting out of transference feelings toward him and did not represent her real feelings. Her so-called feelings of being in love with him were actually a hysterical re-creation of repressed feelings toward her father, a compulsive repetition of the forbidden sexual and aggressive longings toward a father who strictly forbade such behavior toward him. Had the therapist been able to accept these feelings without either giving in to them (accepting them as real) or condemning them, he might have been able to help her to resolve them. Instead, because of his own unresolved oedipal and preoedipal conflicts, he had lost her.

Blunder 9

The Lesbian Therapist
and the Courageous Victim

A woman went to see a therapist who was known to be a lesbian and who only worked with female patients. The patient had recently begun a lesbian relationship, partly as a way of acting out her anger at her husband; she sought out a therapist who would be sympathetic to her plight. The therapist was quite sympathetic, encouraging the patient to leave her husband for her lover and then supporting the woman's efforts to retain custody of her three-year-old son.

"I think you're so courageous to do what you're doing," the therapist would say to the patient again and again. "You're such a beautiful, brave woman. For years you were a victim of your husband's oppression, and now you've stood up for yourself. You can be proud, whatever the outcome." And the therapist would lavish praise on the woman. She also tended to touch the patient frequently, patting her shoulder, rubbing her arm, and hugging her.

The therapist was quite sexually attracted to the patient, who was a lovely woman in her late twenties with blond hair and fine, feminine features. Unconsciously, she wanted to possess her sexually, and she acted out this countertransference by vigorously supporting not only her patient's efforts to separate from her husband, but also her anger at men in general. Eventually, at the therapist's indirect suggestion, the patient broke all personal ties with males in her life, having only minimal relationships with men.

The therapist had never been in therapy and had therefore never resolved her negative Oedipus complex or her penis envy. She had come from a long line of overtly or covertly lesbian women who dominated their passive, covertly or overtly homosexual husbands. Hence her upbringing, in which her mother used the "woman as victim" theme in order to dominate and control her husband, was replete with environmental forces that tended toward the cultivation of homosexuality and hatred of men. Specifically, there was a hierarchy in her family: her mother was contemptuous and demeaning to her father, who was in turn contemptuous and demeaning to the daughter, who was in turn contemptuous and demeaning to her little brother. Meanwhile, the mother was sexually provocative and controlling with the daughter and drew her into an alliance against the father; yet at the same time, her mother was more attached, emotionally, to the younger brother—all of which stirred up unconscious sexual longing and the desire for merger with her mother and, at the same time, resentment and rage at her younger brother and her father.

As a result of this upbringing, the therapist was continually acting out countertransference feelings with her patients, recreating the pattern that existed in her family. In this instance, she kept her patient blocked at a pregenital stage of emotional development, a stage of oral and narcissistic rage (now channeled at men rather than at the bad mother or bad breast). Her unconscious erotic countertransference drove the therapist to guide the patient away from men and toward a lesbian lifestyle, even though the patient was not really a homosexual—the unconscious wish being to possess the patient sexually.

Blunder 10

The Therapist Who Feared His Sexual Feelings

A young male therapist worked for several years with an attractive young female. In the beginning she had poorly established sexual identity, and her femininity was considerably repressed; however, over the course of the years she developed into a woman who was very warm, intelligent, and sexually attractive.

The therapist found himself having fantasies of having sex with her in romantic places, marrying her, buying a house, raising children, and growing old with her. All of these are normal feelings for a therapist to have towards a patient; however, he reacted to them with much anxiety, guilt, and embarrassment, and strove to hide them from his patient. Then, as they began to discuss termination, he discovered that he did not want to let her go. This came to light when, at the end of a session, she expressed her sadness at the impending separation.

"I've really become quite fond of you, and I'm going to miss you," she said. "I'm going to feel sad not seeing you." Tears welled up in her eyes.

The therapist laughed anxiously to hide his own tears, and then remarked rather glibly, "Why do I feel like a mother who has just sent her toddler off to nursery school?"

The patient looked startled; then her brows furrowed, and she was visibly hurt. "You still think of me as a toddler?" she murmured. "That's a bit disappointing."

The therapist had defended against his sexual feelings toward the patient by refusing to acknowledge her as a sexual adult. He had continued to focus on her infantile needs and desires long after they had been resolved in order to avoid seeing how attractive a woman she had become—a woman who could never be his. And in this way he was also unconsciously repeating in the countertransference with his patient the relationship he had had with his mother, who had similarly not wanted to let go of him as a child. The therapist's own mother had, in fact, been quite reluctant to send him off to school and had found an excuse to delay for a year his entrance to the first grade. She had wanted to keep her son at an infantile, dependent stage and wanted to deny her sexual feelings about him.

Such are the cycles that get compulsively repeated in and out of the therapy office.

Blunder 11

The Good Mother and the Bad Mother

In the beginning of the therapy a particular female patient had a very positive transference toward her male therapist, and the therapist in turn had a strong, positive countertransference, responding to her as though she were a "good mother" who appreciated her bright, brilliant son. Her dreams were always about the therapist, her associations were about him, and she seemed to enjoy analyzing her transference and resistance to the therapist. In addition, she often compared the therapist with her husband, complaining about her sex life and speculating on how good she thought the therapist would be in bed.

"You're idealizing me," the therapist would tell her, but on an unconscious level he was eating it up.

Then suddenly things changed. The patient stopped talking about her relationship with the therapist, stopped dreaming about him, stopped fantasizing about him, and spoke incessantly about her husband, asserting that her sex life had suddenly come alive and was wonderful.

All this was experienced by the therapist in respect to his own oedipal situation, so that once again he was the child whose parents excluded him, enjoying themselves sexually and leaving him out. The therapist felt disappointed and angry and reacted now with rage against the patient—the bad mother—and with feelings of inferiority and jealousy toward her husband. The patient, picking up the therapist's anger, reacted by resisting the fundamental rule—free association—so that the therapist's professional pride was also affected, which was a narcissistic blow on top of the oedipal rage. Not only had the patient-mother abandoned him for the husband-father; she also no longer appreciated (fed) him.

The therapist's reaction was all the more intense because of his particular background: his father had come home from a war to a 5-year-old who had grown used to having his mother all to himself. The father proceeded to take the mother away from the boy and to make love to her constantly, sometimes with the bedroom door open. When the boy protested about this, the father mocked him. The mother—a weak, submissive woman—went along with the father. And so the boy remained fixated at the oedipal stage.

Since he had not succeeded in working through these feelings in his own analysis, he was unable to respond correctly to this particular patient.

Blunder 12

To Lie or Not To Lie (On the Couch)

The therapist was an inexperienced young analyst; the patient was an especially attractive, seductive young woman. For a number of sessions they had become deadlocked over the issue of whether or not she was going to lie on the couch.

"Why do you want me to lie on the couch?" she would ask each time he brought it up, a smirk on her face.

Ignoring the smirk, he would reply in as professional a manner as possible, "What's your fantasy? What do you think is the reason?"

"I don't know." She gazed at the couch, turning her head suddenly so that a few strands of her honey-blond hair fell across one of her glistening eyes. "You really want me to lie over there."

"Yes. On the couch."

"On my back."

"Yes. That's the standard way."

She gazed at him out of the corner of her eyes with a knowing look. "Is that the standard way."

"Yes, it is."

The two gazed at one another for a moment, smiling.

"Why is it so important that I lie on the couch?"

"It's not *so* important. You can sit up if you prefer. Lying down speeds things up a bit, that's all. You can do as you like."

"Can I? Thank you. That's nice of you."

"Don't mention it."

The manifest content of each session was whether or not the patient would lie on the couch; however, on a deeper level something else was happening, something that the therapist was not aware of. He was asking her to sleep with him and she was teasing him. It was only after he presented the case to his supervisor that he realized to what extent he was caught up in an erotic counter-transference reaction. Upon hearing a report of the most recent session, his supervisor, an old-guard Viennese psychoanalyst, pounded on his desk and said, "Dees ist not psychoanalysis . . . dees ist love-makingk!" The therapist realized that the emotional content of the therapy relationship with this particular patient was that of courtship, a courtship ritual under the guise of therapy. Each session had the tone and feelings of a tryst between lovers. Both the patient and the therapist were acting out unresolved oedipal feelings without knowing it; thus the therapy had gotten stuck at that place.

Having gotten his control analyst's rather pointed message, the therapist proceeded to begin the real analysis.

Blunder 13

The Therapist Who Feared Love

For a long time a male patient struggled with his tender, vulnerable, infantile feelings towards his female therapist. Finally, one day he began to express them.

"I think I'm . . . beginning to feel . . . well . . . love for you," he blurted out. "I think I'm starting to love you."

There was a long silence. He waited for a response but none was forthcoming. He was a patient who had been abandoned by his mother at an early age, just at the height of his oedipal feelings; he now began to fear abandonment by this therapist.

"Did you hear what I said?" he repeated. "I said I love you."

The therapist paused a while longer, then answered, "Yes, I heard you. That's . . . nice."

"Don't you have a response?"

"What kind of response did you have in mind?"

"I don't know. Something, anything."

In truth, the therapist did not know how to respond, and her silence was felt by the patient to be a form of abandonment. He too lapsed into silence, then went on to a more superficial subject. Inwardly he felt quite hurt; what might have been a significant session had become, instead, a setback to the therapy relation-

ship. It would be many months before he would open up again in
this way.

The therapist had not been able to encourage the patient to
talk of his tender feelings about her, nor to direct him back to this
subject after he had gone to a more superficial topic, because she
was momentarily stunned by the feelings his sudden openness
had aroused in her. She felt very attracted to the patient and was
frightened of these feelings and defended against them by responding in a cold, distant way. The patient had become, at that
moment – on a more primitive level – a longed-for but forbidden
object: he was the oedipal father all at once sexually available.

The therapist was intrigued and curious enough to bring the
situation to the attention of her supervisor, and with her help she
was able to come to grips with the situation. Because this patient
was an exceptional, creative, and sophisticated man, she could
not easily dismiss his criticism of her response. When she realized
to what extent she was attracted to the man, and was hiding
these feelings even from herself, she blushed. At the following
session she was able to acknowledge to the patient that she had
responded in a defensive way when he had opened up to her, and
without going into the reason, assured him that it was her
countertransference problem.

"Thanks for telling me that," he replied. "I really admire
your honesty in admitting your error."

Handling a patient's tenderest, most primitive feelings is
one of the most delicate aspects of doing therapy. A therapist
needs to allow these feelings to be expressed and offer himself or
herself as an object through which the patient can reexperience
and work through early fixations. One must accept these feelings
and not be too hasty in interpreting them as transference, but on
the other hand one has to be careful not to lead the patient on; for
patients who have regressed to the point of developing an erotic
transference neurosis will easily come to believe that a romance
between themselves and their therapists will actually happen,
and need only the slightest sign from the therapist to corroborate

their belief. Then, when such a romance does not occur—as it must not—there will be bitter disappointment on the part of the patient, and the therapeutic alliance will be severely impaired, if not destroyed.

As in the present case, when a therapist is in doubt, a little candor will usually go a long way toward setting the relationship back on track.

Blunder 14

The Seductive Therapist

Before she had become a therapist, she had been a successful actress, both on the stage and on daytime soap operas. However, the very thing that had made her successful as an actress—her beauty and seductiveness—became a handicap to her as a therapist. Since she had never really come to grips with her seductiveness in her own therapy, she was not sufficiently aware of it to be in control of it.

For example, she had a way of looking at certain male patients with a sidelong glance. This glance had become second nature to her; it was the same glance her mother used when she wanted to be ingratiating to her father, and this glance seldom failed to turn her father to jelly. Now this same glance would unwittingly become a source of sexual excitement to her male patients. And there was an unconscious animosity behind this glance, an attitude of contempt toward the male, toward his penis and the male arrogance that, in her mind, it represented. It was as though she were saying in that glance, "Yes, I'm quite attractive, and I know it, and I know what you really want to do to me, you nasty devil, you." These glances would last only a second or two, and she was totally unconscious of their meaning, yet they were quite powerful. And, because she did not know she was doing it, her patients would often feel teased by her.

One young man, typical of many of her male patients, grew angry at her after a while but was unable to articulate his anger. He had had a teasing mother and was, hence, quite sensitive to teasing. He was also susceptible to it. When the therapist would flash one of those glances at him in the course of a conversation, he would feel excited and would think to himself that she was attracted to him and wanted him specially. Then during another part of the session something she would say would indicate to him that she was not sexually attracted to him. As the therapy wore on he became more and more silent, more and more morose.

"You seem angry at me," the therapist said one day.

He sat sullenly, silently in the chair opposite her.

"It seems to be difficult for you to express your anger at me directly," she said.

He glared at her, silently.

Finally, the therapist resorted instinctively to the glance. She shot one at him in an effort to provoke him into words. The glance worked.

"When you glance at me like that," he said, pointing accusatorily, "what does it mean?"

"What do you think it means?"

"It looks . . . well. . . . It looks like a sexual glance to me."

"You're projecting," she hastily replied.

"I thought you'd deny it. That's why I didn't want to say anything."

"I'm not denying. I like you, but I don't feel sexual toward you. At least I wasn't feeling that way at the moment."

"Forget it."

"You feel angry at me?"

"Yes."

"You want to express the anger?"

"No."

The patient spent the rest of the session sitting silently, looking down at the floor, feeling more confused about his perceptions than before he had come to therapy.

Blunder 15

The Negative Oedipus Complex

A young man who was having sexual difficulties with his wife due to unconscious homosexual features in his personality went to see a male therapist who also had unconscious homosexual features that had not been completely analyzed. They quickly formed a very positive therapeutic alliance based on their mutual homosexual attraction for one another. The patient submitted fully to the therapist's suggestions (acting out the unconscious desire to have the father possess him anally), and the therapist responded to this submission with great love (the love for the oedipal father). And so both therapist and patient felt protected against unconscious envy and hatred of their own fathers for having sex with their mothers, and against their anger at each other.

However, as this relationship grew in intensity, and its latent homosexual aspects became more manifest, the wife of the patient became more and more jealous – she became the mother-rival in the oedipal triangle. Hence, the sexual difficulties for which the patient originally sought relief worsened.

Yet, each time the patient would mention to the therapist that his wife was feeling jealous of their relationship, or that his sexual relationship with his wife was becoming less satisfying, the therapist would sidestep the issue by analyzing the wife.

"What do you think her jealousy is about?" he would ask the patient.

"She resents the fact that men can have feelings about one another. She'd like to see men in the stereotypical way, as unfeeling automatons."

"You seem to feel that the problems you're having with her sexually and her jealousy of our relationship are interrelated."

"Yes, I think so. Basically, I think she has problems with intimacy."

In short, the patient and therapist colluded by denying their own aggressive feelings toward the wife–mother–rival, their unconscious desire to exclude her, and their unresolved hatred of women in general. In this instance both the patient and the therapist had had weak and distant fathers and dominating, close-binding mothers who had interfered with their relationships with their fathers. In their present relationship they were acting out a reconciliation with the longed-for oedipal father and a rejection of the overpowering oedipal mother. However, this unconscious acting out of the negative oedipal relationship kept the therapy at an impasse for nearly a year – at which time the therapist came to grips with the problem in his own therapy and in his supervision.

To remedy the situation, the therapist suggested that the patient's wife be invited to a session.

At first the patient was hurt, feeling betrayed. On an unconscious level, it was as though his father had suddenly turned on him and thrown him back to his dominating, hated mother. But the therapist explained, "We've been getting off on excluding your wife, and that's contributed to the problems you're having with her. I felt it might be useful to bring her in for a session to clear the air."

After a lengthy discussion in which the therapist acknowledged his countertransference and how it had led to the impasse, the patient understood and agreed to the meeting. The meeting was a success, and the therapy broadened in scope considerably afterwards.

Blunder 16

The Jealous Therapist

A very pretty, sexually active young woman was in therapy with an older woman who was rather plain in appearance and prudish about matters of dating and sex. Whenever the young woman spoke of her sexual relations with the men she was dating, the therapist would either make a critical comment or attempt to change the subject.

"Do you think I'm promiscuous?" the patient asked one day, sensing the therapist's discomfort.

The therapist paused, then answered, "The fact that you've asked me that question makes me feel that there's a thought in your own mind about your being promiscuous."

"I guess there is. My mother always told me I was too fast for my age. Once she called me a slut when she was angry at me for coming home late."

"So you see me as a judging mother."

"Maybe." The patient was quiet for a moment. "But I also feel that you really do think I'm promiscuous."

"What makes you say that?"

"Well, there have been times when you've made critical comments about my clothes. Once you said, 'That's *some* blouse,' when I was wearing a low-cut blouse. I don't know. It's hard to explain. I just feel that you're judging me."

"I'm not aware of judging you," the therapist replied, and again made allusions to the transference.

The therapist was not in touch with her countertransference feelings of jealousy towards the patient, and therefore she was acting them out (narcissistically injuring the patient) and denying that she was doing so (adding insult to injury). On an unconscious countertransference level, the patient reminded the therapist of the therapist's younger sister, who was much more attractive than she, and who had not only won her father's favor but who had also been very active and popular with boys throughout her teenage years. So the therapist had defended herself against her own feelings of jealousy towards her younger sister by maintaining an attitude of intellectual and moral superiority over her sister, viewing her popularity with men as a kind of sluttishness she herself was above. That situation had now become transferred onto this patient, who actually resembled her sister in many ways.

Unfortunately this therapy situation was not rectified in time, and the patient left after a few months, saying she thought maybe she needed a male therapist. What she was really saying was that she needed a more empathic therapist, and she was right.

Blunder 17

When Parting Was "Sweet Sorrow"

Sometimes a therapist and a patient will "fall in love" for a mixture of reasons, some having to do with transference and others having to do with real factors that make them quite compatible for one another. As Freud and others have pointed out, there is always an aspect of transference in all relationships, in or out of therapy; we can never entirely escape the influences of our pasts.

Such an instance occurred when a woman in her middle thirties, who was married and had two children, entered therapy with a therapist who also was married and had two children. From the first session they were both very much taken with one another. On a transferential level, a twinship transference enveloped them; she felt he was the wisest man she had ever met (the omniscient, nurturing mother), and he felt she was the most beautiful and caring woman he had ever met (the fairy godmother). The patient and therapist both had feelings of low self-esteem, the result of inadequate mirroring during their infancy, and both found in one another simultaneously the adoring parent (the self-object, in Kohut's terms) that neither had ever had.

On a real level, they had many things in common: they were both of Jewish heritage and had both grown up in the same neighborhood in New York City, and they seemed to have a very similar philosophy and have similar interests: both liked foreign movies, opera, seafood, baseball, and the like. More important, both had passive, cold, emotionally inhibited spouses.

The patient was quite open in expressing her feelings of love, need, and sexual attraction for the therapist. The therapist knew he felt the same way. Rather than withdraw into a cold, professional stance, he decided to be honest about his feelings while being clear with her that there was no possible way they could ever act out their feelings. He also discussed the situation with his supervisor, advising the patient that he was doing so.

"I'd do anything for you," the patient told the therapist one day. "If you wanted me to, I'd leave my husband for you. I really would. I've never met anybody I felt so strongly about. And it's not just transference, I really love you."

"I love you too," the therapist replied. "But I'm not at the same place you are; I don't want to end my marriage. And anyway, any acting out physically on our parts would not only be unethical, but might be seriously damaging to both of us. It just really can't be."

On the supervisor's advice, the therapist and patient kept seeing one another until she could find another therapist. They both expressed their mutual regard and admiration for one another—which was beneficial to both of them—and they regretfully planned the termination of their relationship. This included not seeing one another after therapy (this was his decision, not hers, but she abided by it). Parting really was "sweet sorrow" and very difficult and emotionally wrenching for both, but they grew from the experience. They learned that they could indeed be appreciated by a person they respected. In addition, he learned that he could express his genuine feelings toward a patient without being destructive. Both became more self-actualized from the experience, realizing that much of their capacities as human beings had lain dormant due to the regression of their real selves. Thus even though the relationship had to end abruptly, it was nevertheless therapeutic for both of them, and their relationship remained in their memories as one they would always cherish.

Blunder 18

The Patient Who
Felt Like Dying during Orgasm

A young woman went into therapy with a male therapist complaining of sexual difficulties. Although she had a very active sex life, she was never satisfied and sooner or later always found fault with the men she was seeing. Aside from this complaint she seemed to be a fairly well-functioning person, had a good job, seemed psychologically minded, and had an adequate social life.

Her therapist, a psychoanalyst of the classical school, very quickly had her lie on the couch. No sooner had he done so than she began to develop an erotic transference toward him. She began to talk to him about her sexual longings and confessed that lying on the couch made her feel sexual. She confessed, "When I have an orgasm I feel like I'm dying. Have you ever had a patient like that before? What do you think that means?" The therapist felt attracted to the patient and attempted, with difficulty, to analyze the transference.

"What would it mean to you if we had sexual intercourse?"

"I don't know. I don't want to talk about it. I just want to do it. Why don't you come lie down beside me?" She patted the couch with her fingers.

The patient became more and more obsessed with having

sex with the therapist, and more and more demanding about it. She was a woman who, as a child, had had sexualized relationships with both her father and with an uncle; sex to her meant incorporation, fusion, possession. She had always used her sexuality to control and possess men, but then afterwards she was angry at them and rejected them.

The therapist discovered that he was not able to effect a working alliance with this patient, no matter how hard he tried; furthermore, her transference reactions were completely egosyntonic and not subject to self-observation. There was also a desperateness in her proclamations of love for the therapist. What seemed at first to be a sexual come-on became more like an urgent, pressing hunger; it was a last-ditch attempt to cling to her sexual identity and preference and ward off homosexual feelings (she had also had affairs with women, which she found even more dissatisfying than those she had with men). It also seemed that her feelings about herself in general came to rest upon whether or not the therapist accepted her sexually and had intercourse with her.

The therapist felt this desperation and this pressure and became so overwhelmed by her demands that he became confused as to how to handle her. Every session became a struggle; her demands for sex versus his attempt to analyze. She was convinced she needed a "corrective sexual experience" with him, and his attempts to analyze her need was always met by an exasperated sigh, sarcasm, or silence. Eventually he decided, on the advice of his supervisor, to refer her to another therapist.

However, the day he had decided to tell her of his decision, she herself quit, but not before lambasting him.

"Why? You want to know why I'm quitting? I'll tell you why," she told him in an angry but controlled voice. "Because you don't understand women. You're arrogant, if you want to know the truth. I'm sorry, but that's how I feel. I just don't think you know what you're doing. You don't turn down a woman's request for sex. You don't scorn a woman that way. It's just not nice. I don't know. What I really think is that you're a frightened little nerd, and hope I don't ever meet another therapist like you." She did not even finish the session.

Was this therapy relationship salvageable? Perhaps; perhaps not. However, it might have worked if the therapist had not been so hasty to put the patient on the couch. For this particular patient, lying on the couch was far too threatening; she felt it as a seduction, as an invitation to love-making, and when such love-making was not forthcoming, she felt scorned and betrayed. Because of his countertransference feelings – a mixture of sexual attraction and fear and anger – the therapist had a need to quickly take charge of the situation by putting the patient on the couch and throwing interpretations at her in the hopes of quelling his own conflicts. These conflicts stemmed in part from his unresolved needs to regain the love of a mother who had abandoned him for a younger sibling in his early childhood. On the patient's part, she felt the therapist's attempts to distance and control her through the use of the couch and interpretations, and she responded by becoming more resistant, more seductive, and more demanding.

Had the therapist stuck with a more supportive, face-to-face therapy structure, receiving her sexual proclamations in a graceful way without leading her on, being warm and empathic without analyzing, being a good listener and a patient friend until such time as the patient was ready to go further, he might have been able to eventually bring her to the place she needed to go.

Blunder 19

The Sympathetic Therapist and the Schizophrenic Patient

An attractive young woman had a psychotic breakdown following her divorce. During her subsequent hospitalization she lapsed into a catatonic state. The young psychiatric resident who was assigned to her found her very attractive and was quite taken by her. She became his favorite patient, and he spent several hours a day—many on his own time—attempting to draw her out. He would sit on the floor beside her while she chain-smoked cigarettes and gazed stone-faced past him, trying in vain to draw her into conversation.

"How're you doing today?"

Nothing.

"You certainly look lovely today."

Nothing.

"Is there anything I can do for you?"

Nothing.

Because this patient was so withdrawn and forlorn, the therapist found himself wanting to soothe her. On a transferential level, she was his mother, who had herself suffered several breakdowns as the therapist was growing up. Actually, however, it was the therapist who needed to be soothed; he was experiencing the patient's unconscious aggression (her unconscious aggression was inducing anxiety in the therapist), and he needed to do something to relieve this anxiety. In addition he was also experiencing the patient's unconscious sexuality, which she feared and kept repressed (her unconscious sexuality was inducing sexual feelings in the therapist, which in turn was producing still more anxiety). His spending so much time with her was, on an unconscious plane, an acting out of sexual feelings – that is, a kind of courting.

A schizophrenic patient responds to such courting and soothing by withdrawing even further into psychosis; that is, the patient's defenses grow even stronger to guard against the release of aggression or sexual feelings. Hence, in this case the young woman became even more catatonic. Because of his countertransference, the therapist had driven her further inward.

However, by accident, he was able to remedy the situation. After months of getting nowhere with his courting and soothing gestures (feeling once again like the boy whose mother would not respond to his attempts to help her), he became exasperated. One day as he sat next to her he suddenly exclaimed, "Do you talk? Huh? Do you?" His tone of voice was angry now, his gaze challenging. "Maybe you're too stupid to talk. Maybe that's it. Maybe you're just too stupid!"

The patient turned her sensitive green eyes on him for once and, without warning, threw her coffee mug at him, missing his head by a few inches.

"Fuck you!" she whispered, and ran from the room.

In the weeks that followed, the therapist was able to communicate with the patient. By expressing his aggression, he had shown her it was all right to express aggression, and later he helped her to accept her rage and to express it verbally. As she expressed more and more of her pent-up rage, she regained more and more of her capacity to love and relate.

Therapists must be careful not to act out on feelings they are having towards patients, even if those feelings seem to be positive ones such as love, sympathy, or appreciation.

Blunder 20

The Therapist Who Asked for Sexual Fantasies

One day a female therapist asked her young male patient about his sexual fantasies. Although the young man had been in therapy with her for almost a year, he had never talked to her of his sexual life. Most of that time had been spent going through a divorce, so that the therapist had been doing mostly supportive therapy. Now there was more time for analysis, and the therapist asked him about the nature of his fantasies, particularly his sexual fantasies.

"That's embarrassing," he replied. "I've never talked about them to anybody. Not even my wife." He hemmed and hawed and managed to tell her about a recent fantasy, a recurring fantasy that he had when he masturbated: being overwhelmed by an aggressive woman and forced to have an orgasm against his will.

"Have you ever had any fantasies about me?" the therapist asked.

"About you?" He looked at her, blushing.

"Yes." She smiled in a friendly, professional way.

"Why, am I supposed to?"

"Well, it sometimes happens in the course of therapy that the patient has fantasies about the therapist. It's very normal."

"I see." The patient thought about it, and a smirk formed in the corners of his eyes. "Do you want me to have a sexual fantasy about you?"

"Sure."

The young man left feeling elated and puzzled and excited, all at the same time. "This analysis," he thought, "is really something. I'm actually supposed to have sexual fantasies about her while I masturbate—and then tell her about it! This is really exciting stuff." He went home and proceeded to masturbate and fantasize about his therapist—fantasizing that the therapist overwhelmed him and forced him to have an orgasm against his will. Being a therapy novice, he had no idea where all this was going to lead, but he entertained notions that it would actually lead to a real sexual experience of some sort or another with her. Why else would she have him fantasize about her? He was young and narcissistic, a boy–man whose dreams always leapt far ahead of his reality. And his deepest dream, one which lay in the realm of his unconscious, was to regain the love of his mother.

He had been his mother's darling until the age of 4, and she had treated him like a little boyfriend, taking him everywhere with her and confiding in him what a beast his father was. Then, suddenly at four, a little brother was born, and his mother abandoned him for his little brother. He had spent his life looking for the mother who had been his sweetheart before she had abandoned him. Unconsciously, now, that dream seemed to be impending.

On her part, the therapist was unaware of what she had stirred up. Although she knew that it was not generally accepted for a therapist to attempt to elicit an erotic response from a patient, she felt that her therapeutic alliance with this young man was such that she could deviate from standard technique. However, in actuality, she was acting out countertransference feelings toward the young man. A few sessions earlier the young man had been talking about his preference in women, and he had mentioned that he preferred women with small breasts. Then, glancing at the therapist, who had rather large breasts, he said, "I'm sorry, I hope I didn't hurt your feelings." The therapist replied something about "to each his own," but inwardly she was hurt. She had grown up in the footsteps of an older sister who had not only been her father's favorite, but was also one of the most popular among the high school boys. She herself had always been rather plain, with a short, stocky body and thick-lensed glasses. She had worn the glasses since she was 4 years old. In fact, when she had first been forced to wear them, she had suffered a narcissistic blow. Everybody in her family continually complimented her on how pretty she looked with the glasses, but she knew differently. At school she was the butt of many jokes. She had always been jealous of her sister and was sensitive about her appearance.

The patient's put-down of her large breasts (and the implication that he did not find her sexually attractive) rekindled in her feelings of narcissistic and oedipal rage; the patient became, on an unconscious plane, the father who had spurned her in favor of her older sister. Thus, her request that he have sexual fantasies about her was an attempt to force the patient to take notice of her as a sexual being, to see beneath the superficiality of the thick-lensed glasses and the large breasts, to see the inner woman, vibrant and seething with intelligence and wit and beauty.

The patient did just that, and much more. In the weeks that followed he regressed to the age of 4 and began, session after session, to proclaim his love, his admiration, his awe of her. He wrote poems to her, one of which began:

Someday I will hold you,
Still as a star in my arms.
And then at long last
We will merge, we will be one. . . .

At first the therapist was flattered by this attention. Then the attention became increasingly sexual, and the young man persisted over and over in asking her to have sex with him. She was forced, over and over, to refuse him. He became even more adamant, and she became even more stubborn in her refusal. Eventually the young man became exasperated.

"Then why did you ask me to have sexual fantasies about you?" He glared at her. "Why did you do that, if you weren't interested in me sexually? Is it a big ego-boost for you to get me to fall in love with you and then turn me down?"

The therapist denied this and tried to analyze the transference. "It's not really me you're in love with."

"Yeah, yeah, I know. It's really my mother. Whatever you say. The funny thing is, I was never attracted to you in the first place. You . . . brainwashed me into thinking you were attractive. Actually, to tell you the truth, I think you're kind of dumpy."

The therapist tried to interpret his oedipal feelings, the anger at being abandoned by his mother, and his need for a mother surrogate. "What would it mean to you if I went to bed with you?"

"Forget it. I don't want to talk about it anymore."

"How will that help you if you refuse to talk about your feelings?"

"I don't want you to help me anymore. I don't need your kind of help."

The therapy had become deadlocked and remained so for many months. Unwittingly, because of her countertransference, the therapist had recreated for the patient the same seduction-and-abandonment sequence he had experienced with his mother, and his fear, distrust, and anger towards women was reinforced. It would be nearly another year before the therapeutic alliance could be reestablished and any real analysis could take place. Sometimes one mistake can cost years of therapy time and effort.

CHAPTER THREE

SADOMASOCHISTIC COUNTERTRANSFERENCES

Blunder 21

The Lecturing Therapist

A young male therapist had a need to lecture. Whenever a patient did not want to do what he asked, he would give the patient a lecture. Typical of such patients was a young male artist who had gone into treatment because he was blocked. He was a young man in his middle twenties who, like so many others, had come to Manhattan to seek his fame and fortune and had found disillusionment instead. He had not come to therapy to understand himself, but to find out how to get unblocked and to start painting again. The young man had a penchant for complaining and liked to talk on and on about what he was angry about, yet whenever the therapist asked him to do a gestalt exercise designed to help release the anger, the young man refused.

"You know," the therapist said to him one day, "you're not going to get unblocked unless you get rid of your anger. Do you realize how important it is for you to get rid of your anger and to get in touch with the feelings beneath?"

"If you say so," the patient replied apathetically.

"Why don't you pick up that tennis racquet and hit that pillow."

"I don't want to hit that pillow."

"Don't you want to get rid of the anger?"

"Nah. I don't want to get rid of it. I think my anger is important to my creative process. It's my driving force, my power. It's an armor that protects me against the vicissitudes of life. I *need* my anger. I *need* my neurosis. I don't want to get rid of them."

This therapist, like many active therapists, had a need to be helpful. He did not have the patience to wait until a patient was ready for a certain piece of work or a certain interpretation. He was always pushing his patients to get in touch with their feelings. He had both a narcissistic need to be a "great" therapist (each time he could get a patient to do some form of dramatic work, he felt great) and a sadomasochistic need for control and power over his patient. Hence he was unwilling to allow the patient to set his own pace, was afraid of being controlled by the patient, and fought against this fear through activity. If a patient refused to go along with the activity the therapist suggested, then the patient was in for a lecture. On an unconscious level, he was recreating the situation in his childhood, especially during the anal phase, when his own mother used to push him always toward the potty and would lecture him constantly about his habits.

The therapist now lectured the patient about neurosis and creativity. "There's been a long-standing misconception on the part of artists," he said with much authority, "that neurosis is vital to creativity. You're not the first artist I've heard express these sentiments, and you won't be the last. The notion of such artists is that their neurosis somehow makes them special, unique, that it's their 'driving force,' as you put it. But this is really a rationalization, a defense against getting in touch with blocked feelings that the neurotic part of one's personality doesn't want to go near."

"I don't know about that."

"Just sit back and listen a minute. What I'm trying to tell you is that your neurosis doesn't fan the flame of creativity. It may drive you towards fame, but it won't make you more creative. On the contrary, it makes you less creative. It makes you and your work stereotypical, one-dimensional, distorted. Because you're not in touch with your deeper feelings, your work will be shallow and obsessional rather than profound and truly moving. Are you listening?"

"I'm listening."

"The longer you hold on to your anger, the more that anger will poison you. It may feel like an armor, but it's really more a barrier, a barrier that keeps you from any genuine communication with other people. And if you're not communicating with others in an honest way, your perspective of life begins to become more and more biased. The more neurotic you become, the more biased and narrow will be your perspective. The extreme of this, of course, is the schizophrenic, whose perspective has become so biased that it is totally unreal. Are you still following me?"

"I'm following you."

"These feelings of anger that you think are so vital to you and protect you are in reality a self-devised smokescreen. They serve to keep you focused on the external world so that you don't have to feel things inside of you such as fear of death, inner emptiness, and a thousand and one past hurts that have been repressed—going back to early childhood. They keep you from experiencing the full depth of your being, and if you're not experiencing the full depth of your being then you're vastly delimiting yourself as an artist and as a human being."

"Right."

"When a neurotic looks at a particular issue, he or she tends to only see one aspect of it, to take sides, to have a narrow focus. The healthy person sees life in all its complexity and responds to it fully, with compassion and respect for this complexity. What I'm saying is that the popular conception that neurosis is vital to creativity is a myth. Neurosis leads to stagnation and death. Creativity springs from life—from living fully in touch with one's feelings. Do you understand?"

"I understand."

"What do you understand?"

"I understand that you give good speeches."

"What else?"

"I still think I need my neurosis."

"So you're saying you still don't want to work through your anger and get in touch with deeper feelings?"

"That's right."

"May I ask a question?"

"Sure."

"Why are you in therapy?"

"I thought maybe you could give me some pointers on how to get producers to look at my work."

The therapist became increasingly angry at this patient, as he was not able to control him or influence him through his lectures. The angrier he became, the more he pressed the patient to perform for him. Hence he got locked in a power struggle with the patient, and the therapist's very sense of himself became dependent on whether he could "win" the struggle and get the patient to do what he asked. On the other hand, the patient also felt his self-respect was dependent on successfully resisting the therapist's efforts to control and manipulate him—the patient having had an intrusive, controlling mother and an aggressive, bossy father. This power struggle continued until the patient walked out in a huff, leaving the therapist standing in the middle of his office, holding the tennis racquet in his hand.

Blunder 22

The Wolf in Sheep's Clothing

One of a female patient's primary ways of resisting was to be very submissive and very compliant towards her female therapist. She dutifully lay on the couch as soon as the therapist suggested it and free-associated wonderfully. Her free associations were punctuated by submissive little giggles and smiles. She was, indeed, the good daughter.

Her therapist, while consciously aware that this behavior constituted a resistance, was unable to analyze it successfully. Instead, she found herself reacting angrily, suspecting that the patient was attempting to control her and dominate her with this submissiveness. "She's a wolf in sheep's clothing," the therapist thought.

One day the therapist could no longer contain her anger. "You're so very sweet, aren't you."

The patient was taken aback and asked, "What do you mean?"

"I was just noticing how much you giggle and smile. What do you think all that smiling and giggling does for you?"

"I'm not sure what you're getting at," the patient replied, feeling accused and attacked.

The attempt at analysis got no further, and from that point on the patient retreated into a shell. She no longer smiled and giggled (complying with the therapist's indirect request), and she began coming late to her sessions. After several weeks of this the analyst said to her, again, in an angry way, "What do you think your lateness means? Do you have some feelings about therapy?"

"I've been thinking about quitting," the patient quickly responded.

"Let's talk about it," the therapist said.

"I don't want to talk about it," the patient said.

The patient terminated therapy that session.

Upon analyzing, with the help of her supervisor, her intense hatred of this patient, the therapist discovered that the submissive, deceitful part of this patient represented a part of herself, a rejected, split-off part. It was her own desire to dominate her introjected and projected objects that sometimes induced her to adopt a seemingly submissive role: it was the wolf in sheep's clothing which she hated in herself that she also hated in the patient. The patient became the therapist's critical mother, for whom, from the earliest childhood on, she had had to put on a false front, always pretending to be submissive and sweet and good in order to get what she wanted from her, but secretly wanting her dead. So her hatred of the patient was both a fear of the patient's unconscious aggression and of her own.

Blunder 23

The Therapist and the Suicidal Patient

A young female patient who was suicidal was in treatment with an inexperienced therapist who was doing his internship at a clinic. The patient was upset primarily because a dear friend had recently died—one who had represented her "good mother." This was compounded by a particularly abusive relationship she had had, and was still having, with her real mother.

Every now and then this patient would come to a session with a fresh scab on her wrist or forearm, where she had cut herself. The therapist's reaction was always the same.

"Why do you do that?" the therapist would ask, in an exasperated tone of voice. "Why? Why? Why?"

"I don't know," the patient would reply meekly and forlornly.

"I thought we had an agreement that you'd call me if you started to feel suicidal? Didn't we have an agreement?" The therapist shook his head. The patient fell silent. "Can you speak?"

"I don't know what to say."

The therapist was in a rage at the patient, and the patient felt this rage and could not speak. The therapist and patient were locked in a power struggle over the issue of her suicide attempts. Each attempt was perceived by the therapist as an act of spite towards him, while the patient viewed the therapist's demands that she not commit suicide as the demands of her abusive mother.

The therapist. on the other hand, still had unresolved feelings of rage towards his mother, who had committed suicide when the therapist was in his teens. Unconsciously he had hated his mother and wanted her to die, then felt guilty after it actually came to pass. Part of the therapist's unconscious motivation for being a therapist was the need to recreate the situation with his mother; hence he was drawn to suicidal patients. However, now that he had one, he had begun to hate her just as he had hated his mother, and once again this hatred was unconscious.

Unfortunately, this therapist's unconscious hatred, which got acted out through his impatience and demands, finally drove the patient to the brink of suicide. The patient came in for a session feeling quite upset about her mother. Before she left the session, the therapist began to lecture her.

"You're not feeling suicidal, are you?"

"I don't know. I don't think so."

"If you don't tell me the truth, I can't help you."

"I know. I don't know what to say."

"Do you have any pills around the house? I want you to go right home and throw them away. And throw away any razor blades you have around, too. Emily, do you hear me? And call me if you start feeling panicky, okay? Will you promise to call me?"

"I promise."

"And don't just say that and not do it. I mean it. You really *will* call me?"

"Yes, I promise."

Unconsciously the therapist wanted the patient to commit suicide, and his lecturing and demands were, in fact, a kind of indirect induction that would push her to do just that. The underlying message that came through to the patient was that if the patient was not going to be a good girl and do as the therapist asked, then the therapist would disapprove of her. This put the patient in a double-bind situation, just like the ones her mother always put her into. If she did as the therapist asked, she would feel weak for complying with such a nasty and condescending person; if she attempted suicide, she would also be weak and bad. But at least if she attempted suicide, maybe the therapist (her mother) would be sorry for being so nasty to her.

That weekend the patient took a bottle of sleeping tablets and wound up in the hospital on the critical list. She survived, and the therapist was taken off her case the following week.

Blunder 24

The Therapist Who Had To Be "The Boss"

This is how she became a therapist. Three of her children grew up to become heroin addicts, so she enrolled in a local program for parents of heroin addicts. Before long she became a leader of this program. Then, becoming convinced she had special talents in this field, she went back to school to get her master's degree in rehabilitation counseling. Afterwards she attended various workshops on the subject, until she had satisfied herself that she knew everything she needed to know about drug addiction. Naturally, she subscribed to the theory that drug addiction was a disease of genetic origin, having nothing to do with environment. Finally, she set up a private practice in which she specialized in working with people who had drug-abuse problems.

Her practice soon developed into a cult, and her patients became her subjects. While she succeeded in getting them to give up drugs, she at the same time encouraged them to become absolutely submissive to her. They were forced to turn over their salaries to her, and in return she gave them a weekly allowance. They were not allowed to marry, and sexual relations were only allowed with other former drug addicts who were part of her program, and then only under her strict supervision. Her word was always the law, and it became clear to everybody that she was always right. In the guise of being helpful, she was in reality being a sadistic tyrant.

Her need to have her patients completely submissive to her and to be always right was in part her way of defending against the unconscious fear of her own inadequacy; by controlling her patients she was controlling her own fears. In her unconscious, if she was not perfect, if everybody around her did not affirm that she was perfect and accept her authority, that meant complete chaos. This characterological defense had to be maintained in order to ward off the early infantile feelings of rage and splitting as the result of an extremely depriving, and, at the same time, tyrannical mother. The defense was further reinforced when her mother put her in charge of her younger siblings; she identified with the aggressor (her mother) and treated her younger siblings in the same way her mother had treated her. Still later she treated her own children the same way, cultivating a morbid dependency and submissiveness in them.

She was a certain kind of bully—not of the menacing variety but of the subtly castrating sort. She was a large, round woman who gave out an aura of competence and responsibility. Her unspoken message to others was that she and only she really knew how to run things, and therefore she usually had to do things herself if they were to get done right. While this seemed to work well for a while with her patients, since borderline personalities initially need strict boundaries, in the long run she kept her patients at an infantile, masochistic, and dependent level of functioning.

Unfortunately the rigidity of her defenses made her immune to any real supervision. Although she took part in a supervision group, she used the group primarily to "talk at" in such a way as to preclude any real feedback. Once one of the men in the group attempted to offer some criticism of her methods, and she responded by having a temper tantrum.

"I had a feeling about you from the moment you joined this

group," she told the man, trembling with rage. "I said to myself as soon as I saw you, 'He's a woman-hater.' I could see the look in your eyes. You're angry at me because I'm a woman and because my practice is more successful than yours. So you want to put me down, criticize me, humiliate me here in front of everybody. Shame on you. Shame." She shook her finger at him, as though she were his mother, then broke into sobs, "Everybody knows how much I've done for the field, how much I've helped my patients. And everybody knows how hard I've tried with my kids. Do you think it's easy being burdened with three junkies? Do you? Shame on you!" The supervision group rallied around her, the critic was silenced, and the matter was never brought up again.

Blunder 25

The Therapist Who Was Immune to Chatter

For months a male patient lay on the couch chattering away about superficial matters, managing to avoid dealing with his central problems. The therapist, an older man, listened somewhat distractedly to this chatter. He told himself he was bored and distracted because the patient was avoiding, and bided his time. Finally a day came when the patient, during the course of his chattering, began to talk about what had brought him to therapy in the first place.

"You know what I think my real problem is?" he asked the therapist suddenly.

"What's your real problem?" the therapist replied distractedly.

"I'm afraid of abandonment. That's what I think it is." The patient's voice was quite serious and earnest. "I'm really afraid of being abandoned by people I love."

"I see," the therapist replied matter-of-factly.

"You don't seem that interested," the patient said, growing angry. "I've just opened up to you about what I consider the most important problem I have, and all you can say is 'I see'."

The patient, feeling hurt, became desperate and angry, began questioning the usefulness of psychotherapy, and was more and more hostile to the therapist. The patient was especially sensitive to signs of this kind of lack of interest because of his being treated similarly by the significant adults in his early childhood.

On the therapist's part, his countertransference stemmed from a pertinent experience in his own childhood: he had been forced to listen to the endless inconsequential chatter of an elderly grandmother (ordered to do so by his parents, who told him again and again, "Be nice to grandmother, she might not be around much longer"). After a while he felt persecuted by her chatter and developed the habit of being selectively inattentive in order to protect himself from feelings of anger at her and at his parents. Thus, even though he had since been trained to listen in a different way—"with the third ear" as Theodor Reik put it—the present patient elicited from him the feelings he had had for his grandmother. He felt persecuted by this patient's chatter, so he regressed to his former mode of listening and missed the patient's sudden breakthrough.

This blunder caused the formation of the therapeutic alliance to be delayed for several months.

Blunder 26

The Therapist Who Couldn't Say No

A fledgling female therapist was treating a very unstable border-line young woman. She had been told repeatedly by her supervisor that it was important to set firm limits in such a patient. The patient broke every possible rule: she rarely paid and, in fact, had built up a large debt; she was either very late for her sessions or she missed them entirely; she called the therapist at all hours, and the therapist engaged her in lengthy conversations.

The patient became more and more disorganized in the rest of her life. Her repeated absenteeism in her job resulted in her getting fired. She had more and more vicious arguments with her lovers, friends, and family, until she alienated all of them. Despite emphatic warnings from her supervisor, the therapist simply could not draw the line and insist on punctuality, regular payments, and the cessation of telephone calls between sessions. Finally the patient quit therapy, leaving behind a large unpaid bill, but—more important—with her work, love, social, and family life in shambles.

What went wrong? Why did this therapist not follow the rules of treatment of which she was consciously aware? The therapist had a mother who was both verbally and at times physically abusive to her and her siblings. The therapist's mother was such an outrageously tyrannical authority figure that the therapist in no way wanted to be like her. She bent over backwards so far in order not to be like her mother that she ended up at the other extreme, behaving masochistically towards her patient in the guise of being humane. Through her permissiveness, she ultimately destroyed the therapy.

Blunder 27

The Therapist Who Believed in Force

"I don't want you to interpret me," a patient kept telling his therapist. The patient was also a therapist, a therapist of the existential school who didn't believe in interpretations. However, his therapist would not stop interpreting. Each session he would, at some point or another, give an interpretation. This would then lead to an argument.

"I thought I told you I didn't want you to interpret," the patient would say.

"Yes, I know that's what you said."

"Then why are you interpreting me?"

"I feel that's what I need to do as a therapist."

"What you need to do is to follow my cues. If I'm resistant to an interpretation, you shouldn't be giving me any."

"Unless your resistance is a neurotic resistance."

"Neurotic or not, I don't want to hear your interpretations. As a therapist, you should respect my feelings."

"I do respect your feelings, and that's why I keep interpreting. I'm trying to get to your feelings."

"You're getting to my feelings all right. You're getting to my angry feelings."

"That's fine."

"No, it isn't fine. I want you to stop interpreting—do you hear me? I want you to stop. I don't want you to ever, ever interpret me again. If you do, I'll walk out of here."

The two were in a power struggle with respect to interpretations, acting out both anal dominance/submission and oedipal competition feelings. Both therapists were phallic-narcissists with strong sadomasochistic components in their personalities. For the patient, the therapist's interpretations were experienced, unconsciously, as sexual conquests—that is, being anally raped by the therapist (who represented his father); for the therapist, the patient became his tattletailing younger brother, whom he would now eliminate, and his father, over whom he would now triumph.

And, on still another level, the patient represented to the therapist the bad and guilty self he had introjected as a child and now projected onto the patient. By eliminating the patient (interpreting his behavior) he was eliminating his own introjected bad self.

Consciously, the therapist rationalized that he needed to break through the patient's defenses in order to force him to experience his vulnerability. Being of the gestalt school of therapy, he believed in the use of such provocative measures. He was taking the calculated risk that the patient would not leave therapy as he threatened, because he was too involved in the power struggle to leave.

However, the next time the therapist gave the patient an interpretation, the patient was furious. He jumped to his feet and screamed, "I told you! I told you about interpretations, didn't I? Didn't I tell you?" And he threw a folding chair at the therapist and rushed out of the room. The therapist picked up the folding chair and calmly watched the patient leave, without making any gesture to stop him.

That night the patient was having dinner with his wife and another couple. Suddenly, as he recounted his ordeal with the therapist he began to shake, then to feel nauseated. He ran to the restroom and threw up, followed by a case of diarrhea. Then, at last, he sat on the toilet and sobbed like an infant. Yes, he had gotten in touch with his vulnerable feelings, but he was still in a rage at the therapist. He wanted now more than ever to defeat him.

He went back and pretended (perhaps even consciously believed) he had had a breakthrough of lasting significance, that he had seen the light. "You can interpret me all you like now," he told the therapist. For a while things went very well; the therapist gave more and more interpretations, and the patient listened to them and seemed to take them in. Inwardly, the therapist congratulated himself on his innovative method. However, increasingly the patient started to find that he was short of money and asked the therapist if he could owe him. The therapist, feeling they had now formed a good therapeutic alliance, was glad to extend this trust as a show of his appreciation for the patient's valiant efforts. Eventually the patient built up a debt of over a thousand dollars. Then he quit therapy.

"Sorry," he told the therapist matter-of-factly over the phone. "I've made up my mind. I'm quitting. There's nothing you can do or say to change my mind. Have a good life."

"What about the money?" the therapist asked.

"Sue me," the patient replied.

The therapist did attempt to sue the patient, but the patient managed to never be around to accept the summons, and eventually the therapist gave up. At that point he felt quite bitter. Through his unconscious sadism he had only succeeded in causing the patient to be even more resistant to his vulnerable feelings. In addition, he provoked a sadistic counterresponse that had resulted in a painful reversal, not to mention the loss of a thousand dollars.

Blunder 28

Competing with Father

A patient who was himself a therapist was seeing a male therapist who was about ten years younger than he, but who had considerably more experience. The patient complained to his therapist that whenever he was depressed or anxious, his therapist was extremely caring, empathic and effective, but whenever he was doing well, was successful in his profession, and was achieving some status of his own, the therapist was cold, uninvolved, and unresponsive to his achievements.

"I feel as though you're competing with me," the patient said.

"You're projecting," the therapist replied. "You're projecting your own envy of my achievements. In your mind, it is me who envies you, but in fact it's you who envies me."

"I don't buy it," the patient continually repeated. "I think you need to examine your own attitudes more closely."

They went round and round this issue for several months without any resolution, and while they did so the therapy was at an impasse. Finally the therapist began to discuss the matter with his supervisor and with his own analyst and realized that he had indeed developed, and was acting out, a countertransference reaction.

The therapist's father, like himself, had been a very successful doctor. His father had been extremely competitive with the
therapist and unresponsive to his career successes; unconsciously
the therapist had incorporated his father's attitude toward his patient, who was becoming a successful competitor. He was also
compensating through such competitive distancing of the patient
for unconscious infantile feelings he was having toward the patient, fears of being replaced by the patient in the world's (his
mother's) eyes, just as his father had feared being replaced by
him. Seen from a developmental standpoint, this fear of being replaced in his mother's eyes is a manifestation of inadequate mirroring during the oral stage, resulting in feelings of low self-
esteem and a need for personal achievement to bolster those
feelings, with the Oedipus complex being an additional complica-
tion.

In this case, while the therapist's conscious attitude was to
rejoice in his patient's successes, unconsciously – as his father had
done with him – he demeaned him and did not want him to succeed. When he had gained insight into the problem, he confessed
to the patient that there was a countertransference situation.

"I understand," the patient replied. "Being a therapist myself, I know what it's like to get caught up in these things."

Sometimes the therapist–patient dyad can be a healing process for both patient *and* therapist when the therapist truly lis-
tens to what the patient is telling him.

Blunder 29

The Passive Therapist

There was a certain therapist who thought of herself as modern and permissive because she rarely ever made an interpretation. In fact, she rarely ever made an intervention of any kind. She felt that merely listening to whatever the patient said with empathy, now and then reflecting back to the patient his or her statements, was all she needed to do in order to help the patient grow. It was her contention that the patient instinctively knew where he or she needed to go, and that she should let the patient go wherever he or she wanted to go. In short, she allowed the patient to manage the therapy situation completely.

In reality, this therapist's modern and permissive technique was a cover for her masochism. Unconsciously, she was afraid to interpret, afraid to set boundaries, afraid to fight for the patient's integration with his or her unconscious self (in the same way that some parents renounce the responsibilities of parenthood and leave the direction of a child's upbringing to the child and call it progressive parenthood). The therapist was, in fact, exaggeratedly passive and emotionally detached from her patients and was afraid of closeness; to challenge the patient with an interpretation or to make some other intervention might bring about the very closeness she feared. Such intimacy might be *too* satisfying—in her unconscious it would represent a reunion with her pregenital mother, who was controlling and at the same time emotionally depriving. Thus the fear was that the patient would take over and control her. So, while her passivity was, overtly, aimed at giving the patient complete control of the therapy situation, covertly it kept her in control in the sense that it insured that nothing truly intimate or real would occur.

Blunder 30

The Sadistic Group Therapist

A therapist who billed himself as a gestalt therapist had an unusual way of running groups. Upon starting a new group, he would look for the first sign of resistance, viewing it as tantamount to insurrection, and would deal with the resistant individual in a harsh, punitive manner. In this way he would set the tone of the group from the beginning, the tone being, "Do as I say or you'll be out of the group."

For example, a newly formed group was to meet for the first time at 8 P.M. on a certain evening. A male member of the group showed up fifteen minutes late.

"Sorry I'm late," the member said. "I had trouble finding your office."

The therapist looked at the member and smiled sarcastically. "You had trouble finding the office. I see."

"You sound as though you don't believe me."

"What ever gave you that impression?"

The other members of the group laughed as the therapist continued to smile sarcastically at the tardy member. The tardy member began to feel embarrassed and humiliated. "What do you want from me? I said I'm sorry. I promise I won't do it again."

The therapist stared at the tardy member, folding his arms, as if waiting for a confession. The tardy member folded his arms, too. He kept looking away from the therapist's accusatory eyes, searching the faces of the other members of the group for possible support.

"Did you have any feelings about coming tonight," another member asked.

"I was looking forward to coming," the tardy member said. "I just had trouble finding the place. It's as simple as that."

The therapist smiled at the member who had asked the question. Then he stared at the tardy member again, waiting, his arms folded. The tardy member began squirming in his chair.

"I'm feeling a bit angry," he said. "I'd like to go on to something else. I've apologized. I've said I'd come on time from now on. What do you want from me?" The therapist stared at the tardy member, a knowing smile on his face. "Look, I really want this to stop. I'm really getting quite pissed off. I really want this to stop right now."

This interaction went on for another five or ten minutes, with other group members coming to the side of the therapist. Finally, the tardy member became so flustered that he stood up and began to yell that he wasn't going to take this anymore.

"Then why don't you leave," the group therapist said, calmly, smiling.

The tardy member walked out in a huff.

On the surface, the therapist seemed to get good results from this method. Those members who remained in the group had, in effect, become terrorized into complying with whatever he wanted from them. The members literally fell over each other vying for the chance to prove how in touch with their feelings they were. However, they were kept at a submissive level of functioning and never had the opportunity to express or work through their negative transferences. Instead, the group tended to produce obedient individuals who could function well as long as they were in a system in which obedience was a virtue, such as in a corporate setting. However, if individual initiative or an equalitarian relationship was required, they remained at a loss. And as for the tardy member, the treatment accorded him by the therapist and the group was quite destructive to him, causing him to feel shattered, angry, and full of self-doubt for many months. Indeed, the episode was so traumatic to him that he had nightmares related to it for years.

Why did this therapist run groups this way? Consciously he felt he was emulating the founder of gestalt therapy, Fritz Perls. Unconsciously he was acting out countertransference feelings — that is, reenacting a drama that first occurred during his early childhood, when his father, a military man, had him march about the house, stand at attention, and be "summarily dismissed" to his room whenever there was an infraction of the many household rules. His father instilled in him the values of the military ethic, saying to him again and again, "When you grow up, you'll thank me for this." All of this had been introjected and incorporated into the therapist's modus operandi without his being aware of it. He had not worked through his feelings toward his father, and those feelings now got transferred onto his patients. In essence, he had become a dictator/therapist.

Blunder 31

The Therapist Who Aspired to Sainthood

There was a woman therapist who wanted to be a saint and who, in fact, often spoke of "Mother Teresa," viewing the latter as a model of how she would like to be. She saw the therapist's role as one of selfless devotion to the plight of the oppressed. She charged very low fees, let patients build up enormous debts, often gave them extra time and made house calls, and was always supportive and empathic rather than confrontational or analytical. Her patients usually adored her and, indeed, held her up as a saint, and felt profoundly helped by her. However, in reality her "cures" were simply variations of the standard transference cure. Most of her patients remained in and out of therapy with her and dependent on her; she remained their moral arbiter, the star on which they pinned their own fates. Few ever worked through their emotional difficulties or progressed very far along the road of independence and maturity. Here was an instance of a therapist's entire practice becoming an expression of countertransference. How had it come about?

When the therapist was 6 years old, a younger sister was born. The sister had a severe congenital defect that made her sickly and fragile. The family was told that this new sister's chances of survival were very slim. With this in mind, the mother and father were extremely devoted to the younger sister. They spent a great part of their meager funds paying for her medical treatment and, more important, gave practically all their attention to her. The therapist-to-be was pretty much ignored in this process; she was encouraged by her parents to play with the baby and make her possibly short life as pleasant as possible. She was genuinely fond of her little sister and was compassionate about her illness; however, together with these positive feelings – not all of which were reaction formations – she was also jealous of the attention her sister received, angry about being ignored, and aware of wanting the sister to die. Once, while pushing the baby's carriage along a steep hill, she had an impulse to steer it down the hill and into the lake at the bottom of the hill. These impulses frightened her and made her feel guilty, and she felt doubly guilty when her sister died at the age of 2. A part of her rejoiced at this event; another part of her recoiled in horror and disgust at her own "evil" thoughts. As a result, she developed a harsh superego.

When she was in college she was the object of a great deal of attention, both for her beauty and her talent. She played the lead in many college plays and seemed to have a bright future. However, upon graduation she gave all that up as "frivolous narcissistic gratification" and became a therapist. Rather than competing for attention with her sister, her survivor's guilt made her choose to expiate her guilt through the masochistic devotion – and sacrifice of her own needs – to those of her patients. In the end not only did her patients suffer (by being kept at a stage of dependence and immaturity), but *she* also began feeling more and more deprived and angry.

Fortunately she went into analysis and was able gradually to understand the difference between compassion and compulsion.

Blunder 32

The Therapist Who Believed in Catharsis

He was a middle-aged male therapist, trained in psychoanalysis, who nevertheless felt that abreaction was the key to growth. In his work with patients he was always stressing the importance of their getting in touch with their feelings, always pushing for catharses. However, in doing so, he neglected entirely the analysis of the transference. He was of the opinion that once patients got in touch with their feelings, their faulty defenses would automatically fade away, and they would "naturally" develop healthier ways of relating to themselves, their careers, their friends, and loved ones. He prided himself on his short-term approach, rarely working with anybody longer than a year.

One young woman went to him for about a year to work out problems relating to her depression and compulsive eating habits. Using gestalt and primal methods, for several months he got her to scream and cry out her feelings about her early childhood abuse. Then he provided her with supportive therapy for several months after that. To be sure, the abreactive work released much that had been long repressed and went a long way in ridding her of depression. The supportive therapy helped give her the will to control her eating habits. However, in neglecting to analyze her transference, in particular the anal-compulsive and oedipal derivatives that were recreated in her relationship with the therapist, he failed to truly provide her with the insights, skills, and confidence she would need to function at anywhere near her real potential. In essence, he had opened her up and then sent her back out into the world with the suggestion that things would be wonderful from then on.

However, her compulsion to repeat a certain sadomasochistic pattern of relating with the men she dated continued long after this therapy was terminated. Several years later she went back into therapy, this time with a psychoanalyst, to work through this problem.

This first therapist took a dim view of analysis because he was the son of a psychoanalyst, a woman who used to analyze her son throughout his childhood in such a way as to continually manipulate and intrude on his personal life. In his own training analysis, he picked a senior analyst who, like himself, found reasons to dismiss the analysis of the transference: his unresolved feelings about his mother and how they affected his present relationships were largely ignored or glossed over. In addition to this, the therapist had never worked through his fear of intimacy. By refusing to analyze the transference, he was keeping the patient at a distance (just as his mother had kept him at a distance). Thus, in performing therapy the way he did, he was merely acting out his countertransference feelings, recreating his own compulsion to repeat, at the expense of his patients.

Blunder 33

The Therapist
Who Was Concerned about Money

At the start of a session a patient wanted to pay his monthly fee. He gave the therapist a thousand dollar bill and asked for change. The therapist had to go into another room to get his money, leaving the thousand dollars on his desk. While he was gone, the therapist had a fantasy that the patient would take the money back and say that the therapist took it. His fantasy—an expression of countertransference feelings aroused by the patient—was based on what he already knew about the patient, who had previously shown a strong disinclination to pay his fees. In addition, this patient now had a negative transference toward the therapist that consisted of a recreation of the negative relationship he had had with his father. Finally, this particular patient also had a psychopathic component in his personality.

The therapist knew that the fantasy was valuable because it indicated to him what the patient was feeling—in the course of therapy, or any long-term relationship, the two unconsciouses of the dyad become connected by a symbiosis. Thus, when the patient has thoughts and feelings, the therapist (when he is in tune) will have corresponding thoughts and feelings. The therapist presumed that the patient was thinking about taking the money and that he actually might do so.

When he came back into the room the money was still there. He gave the patient his change, and the patient lay on the couch and was silent. The therapist waited for the patient to admit that he had thoughts of taking the money. Instead, the patient went on to other matters. The therapist became angry.

"Did you have any thoughts or feelings about the monetary transaction between us just now?" he finally asked.

"Not really," the patient replied.

"Let me ask you," the therapist continued. "Did you have any feelings about my leaving the thousand dollars on my desk and going into the other room."

"Not really."

"I had a fantasy while I was out of the room that you'd take the money and then say I took it."

"Are you saying you think I'm a thief?"

"I'm just wondering if you had any such thoughts."

"Not at all. Actually, I feel hurt that you'd think such a thing."

The therapist had narcissistically wounded the patient and damaged the therapeutic alliance. His initial reaction to the situation had been quite correct—he had wanted to use his countertransference feelings to interpret the patient's behavior. However, by not waiting for the patient to volunteer the information, by attempting to trap him as though he were on the witness stand, he only succeeded in antagonizing him. He had acted out, rather than effectively utilizing, his countertransference feelings. The therapist had become so angry at the thought that this patient was trying to rob him that he began to perceive the patient as a persecutor: that is, he took on a masochistic stance, and his own anal-retentive character traits rose to the surface. Unconsciously, he feared the return of his own repressed pregenital rage and guilt and acted compulsively (through overaggressive interpretation) to head off this fear.

Blunder 34

The Therapist Who Got Married

When a fairly attractive and young female therapist got married, one of her male patients became upset.

"This is so, so sudden," he said. "You never even *mentioned* anything about seeing anybody, much less being engaged. I don't know how to feel about this. I really don't."

The therapist smirked at him. "You feel jealous, is that it?"

"I don't know," he snapped, looking away from her. "I'm just shocked, that's all."

A few sessions later he informed her that he was going to have to leave therapy because of career considerations. When she attempted to discuss it with him, he refused to do so, saying that it was simply a practical matter and nothing else. He terminated with that session.

What happened? Unconsciously the therapist had taken a narcissistic pleasure in this male patient's erotic transference to her and his need to idealize her. Hence, she had unwittingly led him on, not in any direct way but by a subtle flirtation with him. Then, when she saw how upset he was by her getting married, she experienced a sadistic satisfaction in her power over him, again quite unconscious on her part. However, the patient felt both the leading on and the sadism and responded to it by terminating therapy.

Blunder 35

The Defensive Therapist and the "Guilt-Tripping" Patient

A middle-aged woman had had a cruel father and had undergone a series of tragedies in her life. However, rather than attempting to overcome these tragedies, she used them in a subtle, complaining way to elicit sympathy from whomever she was with. Her masochistic character kept her stuck in the role of victim, a role she had learned from her mother. Both her mother and she were subjected to the tyranny of her father, and they formed, early in her childhood, a mutual "crying dyad," thus uniting against the common enemy and receiving solace from one another.

In fact, the patient's life story was so horrendous that the initial recounting of it could never fail to elicit sympathy. It was replete with emotional and physical abuse, usually at the hands of the men in her life. However, she was getting so much mileage out of being miserable that she would not give up her misery or ever make any serious attempt to correct or transcend her situation.

When she was referred to a male therapist by a woman friend who was also a therapist, she told him her story and he, like everybody else, was at first very much moved by her plight. However, after a while he found himself pressing to get her to see her repeating pattern.

"You know," he told her one day. "You seem to me to be almost aggressive about being a victim."

"What do you mean?" she demanded.

"I wonder whether there's a part of you that enjoys being a victim, that gets off on being a victim."

"Gets off on being a victim?" She gazed at him, agasp.

"Yes, in a way I think you do." The therapist went on to explain to her how she got off on being a victim, and she continued to gaze at him in disbelief. Although the therapist's interpretation was correct, his timing was off. She was obviously not yet ready to hear what he was saying. As a result, from that point on she began to behave towards him differently than before; her tone and manner told him that she was deeply offended by him, and that he himself, through his interpretation, had now become still another person, still another man, who had victimized her. The two became locked in a struggle: she began more and more to try to make him feel guilty, and he reacted by becoming more and more defensive, reiterating his interpretation and refusing to back off from it. She had a sweet, subtle way—never directly confronting or attacking him—to make him feel like an insensitive brute who did not have compassion for her suffering. He would, in turn, take an exasperating, patronizing tone towards her.

The patient's method of inducing guilt aroused in the therapist strong feelings of anger related to his mother. He had had a mother who operated in almost the exact way as this patient. Rather than the "I'll put my head in the oven" or "You'll give me a heart-attack" routines, his mother had induced guilt in him in the same way the patient did—through a subtle accusatory sweetness that always enraged him. He handled this patient the same way he had handled his mother—utilizing a defensive posture of subtly patronizing her.

Eventually the power struggle was broken when the patient called the friend who had referred her to this therapist and had her intervene. The friend helped the therapist to come to grips with his countertransference, and he was able to resume the therapy relationship in a way that allowed him to back off from the power struggle and be sympathetic to the patient. Once that happened, he was able to help her move beyond her masochistic pattern and effect some positive changes in her life.

Blunder 36

The Condescending Therapist and the Multiple Personality

A female therapist, who was somewhat renowned because she had published several books, was pompous and condescending to her patients. Unconsciously, she saw them as inferior beings, and this attitude was transmitted despite a great show of caring and concern. As a result, her patients never completely opened up to her.

One patient, for example, was a multiple personality. She saw this therapist for a year and at one time or another each of her seven personalities attended a session. However, these personalities never trusted the therapist enough to reveal themselves to her. The therapist, viewing the patient as she did through a veil of pomposity, misdiagnosed the latter as a manic-depressive – one of her personalities was quite manic and another depressed – missing entirely the range of behavior represented by the other personalities, one of which was relatively healthy. As the result of her misdiagnosis, she put the patient on a psychotropic drug (an antidepressant) that was wrong for her and caused her to have anxiety attacks and adverse side effects. Her interpretations were also off the mark, since she did not really "see" the patient.

Although the patient, like many, had gone to the therapist because of her renown and had, therefore, developed an instant positive transference toward her, nevertheless there was hardly any real progress during her year with the therapist. Yet she often pretended to feel and think the way the therapist wanted her to feel and think in order to win the therapist's approval.

This therapist in reality had very little self-respect. She had completely split off her "bad self"—her preoedipal feelings of rage, jealousy, and low self-esteem—and defended herself from them through the cultivation of an ideal image of herself as good, noble, and righteous. Her books, full of therapy successes, were an attempt to rationalize this ideal image. At the same time, she projected her "bad self" onto her patients; *they* were crazy, and *she* would save them. So her mother had done to her as a child; and so now she did to her patients.

As a writer she was brilliant. As a therapist she was less than adequate. And her very pomposity precluded her having the kind of therapy or supervision that might help her overcome these deficiencies. Such is sometimes the price of success.

Blunder 37

The Guilt-Ridden Therapist and the Accusatory Patient

The patient was a young woman who had had a great deal of difficulty in her relationships with men. These relationships had been characterized by much sadomasochism. The patient was basically a paranoid masochistic character, a "professional victim," who anticipated being done in by men and so would set out to make this scenario a self-fulfilling prophesy. She would do this by picking at minor transgressions as proofs of a man's evil intentions. These accusations over a period of time, along with other provocative behavior, would eventually cause the man to become so enraged he would reject her. Naturally, the patient began to see evil intention in her male therapist after a while.

"That's a sexist remark," she would frequently say to him. "In fact, just about everything you say is sexist. What you really want to do is debase me. You don't see me as a human being. I'm just an object for you to control and debase and humiliate."

The therapist, who had worked on his own sadomasochistic relationships in his therapy, became outraged at her generalization that he was a male chauvinist. "What have I done to show you that I'm a chauvinist? Just tell me one thing I've said or done?" he asked, attempting to constrain his anger. "Come on, tell me."

"I can't tell you one thing. Practically everything you say is sexist."

"Well, I don't agree with you."

"Fine, you don't agree. Where does that leave us?"

"You tell me."

"No, you tell me. You're the therapist."

The therapist became more and more involved in an angry sadomasochistic relationship with the patient, in which she would put him on the defensive through one of her accusations and he would attempt to defend himself. She had sucked him into the same pattern she had displayed with all the men in her life.

The therapist recounted the situation to his supervisor, feeling that all was lost. The supervisor analyzed his countertransference, observing that the therapist's mother had been a guilt-provoking woman much like the patient, a woman he could never please. The therapist had taken in the guilt and had, at the same time, repressed the rage over his mother's guilt induction. Now this rage had been rekindled in the present therapy relationship. The supervisor suggested that the therapist acknowledge to the patient that their relationship had followed the same pattern that she had had with other men, and that he had unwittingly got sucked into the pattern.

The therapist did as the supervisor suggested and, having resolved his countertransference guilt, he was able to help the patient examine her modus operandi without getting involved in a power struggle; hence they were able to search together for the roots in the patient's childhood that led to her destructive pattern.

Blunder 38

The Masochistic Therapist
and the Hostile Patient

A young man was in therapy with a male therapist who was about his same age. The young man had a close-binding mother and a somewhat dominating father. The father had taken complete charge of the boy's toilet training and acted out his repressed infantile feelings by attempting to make the boy feel inadequate. The boy responded by soiling his pants for several years. Later, the father had the boy work with him in the fields (he was a farmer) and would again make the boy feel inadequate. He would ask the boy to do a chore, but before the boy could even get started, he would grab the tool away from him and do the chore himself, saying, "You'll just fuck it up as usual."

In his relationship to the therapist, the young man – the boy grown up – began treating the therapist as though the therapist were inadequate. He had taken the defensive position of identification with the aggressor (his father), while projecting his own feelings of inadequacy onto the therapist, playing out the childhood scenario in reversal. He was continually asking the therapist to try new therapy techniques on him. The therapist, being masochistic and not wanting to say no to the patient, would invariably comply. The patient wanted to try bioenergetics. The therapist complied. The patient wanted to try gestalt therapy. The therapist complied. The patient wanted to try hypnosis. The therapist complied. Each time, however, the patient found fault with the therapist's technique. He was never good enough for the patient. The therapist eventually stopped complying and became angrier and angrier. He expressed his anger at the patient through interpretations presented in an angry tone of voice. The patient responded by rejecting the interpretations, sometimes laughing at them contemptuously.

"Sometimes I think maybe you're not the right therapist for me," the patient would often say.

"Why's that?" the therapist would ask wincingly.

"I don't know. I don't mean to hurt your feelings but, well, sometimes I wonder if you're smart enough for me."

"What makes you think I'm not smart enough?"

"Well, for one thing, your interpretations are so off-the-wall. And, for another thing—I hope you won't take this personally—for another thing, I don't know if you know what you're doing. I mean, you keep using all these techniques, gestalt, hypnosis, bioenergetics, and I don't think you've really had enough training to do them properly. And also, I don't know, I just don't think you're smart enough to handle me. You're always getting mad at me. I can tell when you're mad. You get silent. Like you are now."

The therapist was indeed very silent and very "mad." He could scarcely constrain his anger for the remainder of the session.

This therapist had been the scapegoat of his family; his older brothers and sisters as well as his parents had constantly made him the butt of their jokes as he had grown up, and since then he had gone through a series of sadomasochistic relationships with women and with men. Now he had come to perceive this patient as a ridiculing older brother or sister. He became more and more obsessed with the patient, even to the point of having fantasies of revenge (the kinds of fantasies he use to have about his family). He could not focus at all on any of the patient's good qualities nor be empathic about the patient's negative transference toward him. Although on a conscious level he understood the transference, still he had no sympathy for the patient.

One day the patient came in with a new request. He wanted to know if the therapist would give him an honest opinion: Did the therapist think the patient was ready for termination? The therapist paused, then offered the opinion that the patient was not ready and gave reasons why. The patient seemed to listen, then rejected the therapist's opinion saying, "I disagree with you completely. I really don't think you know what you're talking about. Starting next week I think I'll just come one session a week instead of two and see how that goes."

"If that's what you want to do," the therapist replied.

"That is what I want to do."

The therapist felt defeated, tricked, tortured by the patient. He thought about him all weekend, even having sleepless nights. The following Monday he went to see his old supervisor, and the supervisor recommended that he terminate the patient. At first the therapist did not want to do so, for he did not want to admit failure. He had become so locked into the power struggle with the patient that, in his mind, terminating the patient not only meant failure, but also that he had lost and the patient had won (i.e., his older brother had won). However, the supervisor prevailed, and the therapist greeted the patient at their next session with the suggestion that they terminate.

"I think perhaps you were right about me," the therapist said. "I think maybe in a way I'm not smart enough for you."

"Are you being sarcastic?" the patient asked.

"No, I mean it. I think I wasn't experienced enough to handle you, and I'd suggest that you find a therapist who's more experienced than I am. I'd recommend one to you, but I don't know if you trust me enough to take my recommendation."

"That's all right," the patient replied standing up. "I'll find my own."

The therapist thus ended the relationship in an honest way and then went back into therapy himself to work through his own unresolved masochism.

Blunder 39

The Solicitous Therapist
and the Suicidal Patient

A female therapist was treating a young woman who was going through an extremely difficult period. At times she was despondent and would speak about suicide, though in fact she was not really a suicidal character.

"I don't know," she would mutter in a weak voice. "Sometimes I think maybe I should just kill myself and get it over with. Everything seems so futile, so bleak. I wake up in the morning, and I don't even want to get out of bed. I mean, what's the point? Everybody hates me anyway, so I'd be doing them all a favor."

The therapist became extremely anxious and obsessed about the patient. Even though consciously she realized the patient was in fact not in danger of attempting suicide, she began to worry about her constantly and had trouble sleeping at night. She insisted on extra therapy appointments and began calling her at night to inquire after her state of mind. The therapist recognized that her behavior was not in the best interest of the patient—nothing will drive a potential suicide to the brink more than over-solicitousness—yet she could not stop herself. Finally, because of her reaction to this patient, she went back into therapy and supervision.

The therapist had had a younger sister who had severe and chronic emotional problems. Her mother often left this sister in the therapist's care, and the therapist was always fearful something terrible would happen to her younger sister and she would be blamed. She was oversolicitous to her sister as a defense against her desire to get rid of her. Her sister's birth, when the therapist was only two years old, was a narcissistic blow to her, for at that time she felt abandoned by her mother and retreated into herself. On an unconscious plane she decided she must not be very good if her mother could abandon her that way and that the younger sister was more valuable than she was. Now, in the same way, the therapist had an unconscious sadistic desire to get rid of the patient and responded with the same solicitousness she had displayed toward her sister. And she had the fear that, if the patient died, she would be blamed and would be sued for malpractice.

The therapist was not able to work through these issues quickly enough to be of help to this patient, so fortunately she was able to recognize this and refer her to another professional. In some cases, that is the best solution for both parties.

Blunder 40

The Therapist Who Sexually Abused His Patient

A 28-year-old woman was in therapy with a nationally known therapist for six years. During the last few years of their relationship he was seeing her regularly outside the office, and their sexual affair had decidedly sadomasochistic features. For example, he would tie her up, beat her, and sodomize her. During this period she continued to see him in his office and to pay for her regular psychoanalytic sessions.

The patient was also in a group with this therapist. He told her to never tell group members that she was involved with him sexually, but to talk about him and her reactions to him using another name for him in the group. He also warned her that if she told people in the group that they were sleeping together, it would have a bad effect on her "siblings" and might precipitate a psychosis or a suicide attempt in one or more of them. In addition, he threatened that he would have her committed as being psychotic if she divulged the nature of their sexual involvement.

The patient was a bright, relatively healthy young woman; she had some neurotic symptoms that had led her to enter therapy, but she was neither psychotic nor even borderline in character. Aside from this one relationship, she had never had a sadomasochistic affair. She was quite successful in her profession.

Eventually this patient became so confused and upset that she consulted another therapist.

"I feel so . . . so stupid," she told him in a barely audible voice, her eyes gazing forlornly at the floor. "I feel so stupid to . . . to have let all this happen to me. How could I do this to myself? How could I let him demean me this way? I don't understand it. I really don't understand it."

"Are you feeling angry at him?" the therapist asked.

"No . . . no, not really. I don't know what to feel. I suppose I know, intellectually, that I should be angry at him. But I'm not." She glanced up awkwardly, then gazed back at the floor. "In many ways he's been helpful to me. In fact, I feel I'm betraying him right now, by coming here to you. I blame myself for being so stupid. And I'm so scared."

"Scared?"

"Scared to get involved again. I just . . . I just don't know if I can do it. I'm afraid if I get involved again the same thing will happen."

The consultant referred her to a female therapist, and with the help of the female therapist the patient began a long process of recovering her sense of self. After a while she was able to break away from the abusive therapist and to once again assert her boundaries with the men she was seeing; however, it took many years of hard work.

And what of this therapist? How did he get that way? Are there many like him?

Obviously the therapist was acting out a sadomasochistic countertransference of the most vicious kind. Unfortunately he was a therapist who had gone to the best schools, been trained in a prestigious analytic institute, had undergone a rigorous training analysis and supervision, all without making a dent in his emotional pathology. This therapist had, as a young child, been sexually abused by his mother. She had, for example, attempted to toilet train him before he was emotionally ready, and when he resisted she would physically grab him and hold him down on the toilet for hours, until he moved his bowels. If she had to go away, she would tie him to the potty. He would cry and scream to no avail; in fact, she would laugh at him when he did so. In retaliation, the boy began to soil his pants. He kept soiling his pants throughout his oedipal years, and she in turn started giving him punitive enemas. Every time she would find a lump in his pants, she would pull his clothes off and throw him onto his bed and "rape" him with the enema apparatus. As the result of all these and other abusive happenings in his childhood, this therapist contained the seeds of cruelty inside him, and this cruelty got taken out on his patients.

Although this kind of therapist is rare, we did not feel a book such as this one would be complete without including one such case. Also, it brings up an important question: how did such an intelligent, successful, and relatively healthy patient succumb to this outrageous exploitation? Why did she remain with an abusive therapist for years without recognizing she was being exploited and misused? Why did she wait so long to do anything about it? The explanation for this phenomenon is that therapy fosters regression to a first-year-of-life level of ego development. This is not only a regular occurrence, but also a desirable one: it is when a patient is regressed that the most important abreactions and analyses of the transference and resistance occur. However, during this period of regression there is a reappearance of the infantile wish to fuse with another human being (the omniscient mother). This mechanism has been observed in hypnosis, and it clearly occurs frequently in analytic and other forms of therapy as well. Kleinian therapists and object-relations therapists assume this development with all their patients; some of their interpretations are based on this expectation. In this regressive state ego boundaries are loosened by the therapeutic process, and the ego is extremely susceptible to invasion by another person. The patient is, so to speak, "thrown into a trance" and is at a tremendous disadvantage as far as her ability to use her adult faculties to protect herself against a therapist who wishes to invade her or misuse her.

In this case, the patient could no longer distinguish between her own wishes and impulses and those of the therapist. Suggestions that belonged to the therapist began to be experienced as her own; but she concurrently experienced an unclear definition of herself, her own wishes, and her own boundaries. During the course of therapy it got to the point where she could no longer experience herself as separate from her therapist, and was therefore unable to experience any hostility towards him that was not immediately redirected against herself. This brainwashing continued until she became a "zombie" in relationship to the therapist, while she maintained relatively good ego functioning with respect to the rest of the world.

These symptoms of zombie-like behavior, confusion, symbiosis, are so specific to this experience that a specific diagnosis might be in order for it: *iatrogenic psychiatric illness,* that is, a psychiatric disease caused by a psychiatrist. This is a syndrome that can be described as clearly and in as circumscribed a manner as other syndromes found in medicine, psychiatry, and psychotherapy. It is a malady that has more to do with the psychiatrist's treatment of the patient than it does with the patient's own psychopathology.

CHAPTER FOUR

NARCISSISTIC COUNTERTRANSFERENCES

Blunder 41

The Therapist and the Skeptical Patient

"I hope this works out, but I can tell you right now I'm skeptical," the patient said on his first interview. He was somewhat nervous looking, with flickering fingers and intense, dark eyes that bore down on the therapist.

"Why do you say that?" the older, male therapist asked.

"Well, the same man—a friend of mine who's a therapist—who referred me to you also referred me to another therapist, the one I just left. I saw her for a year and a half and I don't feel she ever really cared about me. I mean, she'd pretend to care about me; you know, she'd act real professional and all. But then she'd suddenly make some comment that would blow my mind. I mean every time I was about to trust her, she'd pull the rug out from under me." The young man provided this new therapist with a list of examples of how this previous therapist had failed him. Then he paused and stared at the therapist who sat silently before him. "This same man who referred me to her now referred me to you. I'm wondering if I can trust you."

The therapist was silent a moment, but in the pit of his stomach he felt a tugging. He was compelled to defend himself and to assuage the patient's feelings.

"This is a completely different situation. For one thing, I'm a male therapist, and she was a female therapist. And we have different methods of doing therapy."

"I know, but . . . still, the same guy referred you both. What if he made another mistake."

"Just because he made one mistake doesn't mean he'll make another one. Did you tell him about the previous therapist? Did he understand what went wrong, and what kind of therapist you were looking for now?"

"Yes, I think so. But you can never tell. I told him what I was looking for before, too, and he sent me to her. I told him I wanted somebody who cared, somebody empathic–and he sent me to her! Now he said you'd be empathic, but I don't know. You seem empathic, but. . . ."

"Most patients do find me empathic. I don't usually have any complaints on that score."

The therapist continued to mollify the patient and to try to win his approval in the next few sessions. He found that the more he did so, the more skeptical the patient became. Hence, the therapist began feeling more and more anxious. He began to dread the patient's weekly appointment and anticipated that the patient was going to leave him.

Luckily the therapist was able to use his anxiety as a signal that something was awry. In discussing the situation with his supervisor he understood his countertransference. The therapist's father was a prominent therapist who had been consistently and subtly disparaging of his work. This new patient was also a therapist-in-training, and by taking a skeptical position from the beginning, he had put the therapist on the defensive. The patient became, on a transferential level, the therapist's critical father, whose approval he would not be able to win.

"Losing this new patient might be disappointing," the supervisor pointed out, "but hardly a matter of life or death. On the other hand, when you were a child and you were dependent on your father, losing his approval was a matter of great moment."

Indeed, when the therapist had been a child, his father had been absolutely cold and disapproving, and the boy had developed a tremendous amount of castration fear. His mother, while overtly caring, was too submissive to the father to be able to comfort the boy. Now, in his adult life there was an unconscious, latent desire to win the approval of important males in his life.

As the therapist became aware of this negative Oedipus complex and how it, along with unfulfilled narcissistic needs, contributed to his need to mollify this patient, he was able to rectify the situation. The next time the patient expressed his skepticism about whether the therapist would care about him, the therapist replied, "There is certainly the possibility that I won't be able to care about you. There's always that possibility. But there's also the possibility that you're setting up a situation here."

"What do you mean?" the patient asked, and his fingers were flickering a bit faster.

"Perhaps you want unconsciously to set it up so that I don't care about you. Perhaps that's your repeating pattern. You want to set it up so that I don't care about you so that you can justify rejecting me."

The patient, being a therapist-in-training himself, was able to take in this interpretation. "I see what you mean." His fingers stopped flickering, and he nodded emphatically. "Yes, that makes sense. I see that. I've never felt cared about. I never felt cared about by my parents, so I could see how I could look for people not to care about me and set it up that way. Yes. Yes."

The patient had begun the working-through process.

Blunder 42

The Infantilizing Therapist

"I have something to ask you," a 25-year-old homosexual man asked his female therapist after the third or fourth session. "I was wondering if you, well, if you would mind giving me a hug at the end of our sessions."

After going through standard psychoanalytic procedure with him, asking him what it would mean to him, she replied, "I suppose it would be okay."

The patient's father had divorced his mother when he was seven years old. At that time his older brother, who was very successful and responsible, had taken over his father's role. The patient, on the other hand, was "Mama's baby." She slept in the same bed with him into his teens and generally overprotected and infantilized him. Despite considerable talent and intelligence, the patient had drifted throughout his adult years.

The therapist found she had strong feelings for the patient of a sexual-maternal variety. One of the therapist's major dynamics was that she had been a "fag's hag," a woman attracted to homosexual men. In her own analysis she had traced this attraction back to an infantile, omnipotent wish to change a man's sexual preference as a proof of her feminine power. Her father had admired her "masculine" qualities but never her "feminine" ones, while her mother was competitive with her. Hence she was quite insecure about her attractiveness as a female. Now she found that she had a strong desire to change this homosexual patient to a heterosexual male by getting him attracted to her. Thus the hugs she gave him at the end of each session were in the service of her narcissistic grandiosity. And, naturally, they only brought about more regression and kept the patient dependent and infantilized, while her desire to change him, which he unconsciously picked up, produced a strong resistance to such a change and a resentment at not being accepted on his own terms.

Blunder 43

The Protective Therapist

A pretty young female patient spoke rather matter-of-factly to her male psychotherapist about having been seduced and abandoned by a man the previous weekend. It was a typical case of a man waxing warm and romantic and loving until he had gotten the woman in bed, and then disappearing the next day with an arrogant smile on his face. To top it off, he had called her a couple of days later to tell her he had decided to leave the city and move west.

"What did you say to him when he told you that?" the therapist asked.

"I said I'd miss him," the patient answered in her matter-of-fact manner, shrugging her shoulders.

"How were you feeling?"

"Sad."

"Just sad? Nothing more?"

"No. Just sad. Why?"

The therapist found himself feeling angry at this man for leading his patient on, and he suddenly blurted out, angrily, "You should have told him, 'Good-by, jerk, and good-riddance!'"

He had formed a narcissistic countertransference identification with her and had acted out on it; the intensity of his reaction and his behavior were harmful to the therapeutic situation, causing the patient to feel even more inadequate. He was swept out of his analytic role by his protective feelings for the patient and a hatred of deceptive people, both rooted in his past. This led him to identify with the patient's predicament and to respond with a narcissistic rage, as though he himself had been rejected.

"I guess I *should* have said that," she replied morosely. "I really am stupid sometimes. I never think of those things."

"No, I don't think you're stupid," the therapist quickly responded, regaining his composure.

"Yes, I am."

"It's hard to think of what to say when you're feeling hurt."

"No, I'm just stupid," she said, retreating further and further into a masochistic stance, hugging herself, gazing downward. "It's just me; I'm too stupid to say the right thing. I always was and I always will be."

Blunder 44

Pushy Mothers and Pushy Fathers

A male patient was talking to his female therapist about his feelings about his 8-year-old son. "I want him to do all the things I was never able to do," he said plaintively. "I want him to make good grades—and I mean A's, not A-minuses—and I want him to be a star in little league, and I want him to take piano lessons. But he keeps fighting me all the way. I don't know what I'm going to do with him." The patient, who was quite narcissistic, was obviously attempting to live his life through his son.

As the therapist listened to him she became angrier and angrier. She felt her body tighten up, and her throat was also tense as she made what she thought was a neutral comment: "You seem to want a lot from your son."

"Yes I do. Is that bad? You seem upset."

The therapist's mother had been an extremely narcissistic woman, a would-be opera singer who had a need to control and dominate everyone around her, especially her daughter. She had once told the therapist, "You're my right arm." She wanted her daughter to be the opera star she had never become and constantly pushed her in that direction—while at the same time sabotaging the therapist's operatic ambitions, since unconsciously she did not want to be surpassed by her. When the therapist heard her patient talking in much the same way about his son as her mother had talked about her, her rage at her mother was revived.

When she discussed the situation with her supervisor and understood her countertransference, she was able to transcend her anger and give the patient the same interpretation but with an empathic tone of voice and body language instead of the angry, critical one. In response, the patient was able to hear her.

"Yes, I do seem to want a lot from my son. Perhaps I want too much. Is that what you're saying? Perhaps I'm living my life through him? Oh, God, I never thought of it like that. You know, I think you're right. I think I really am."

Blunder 45

The Self Psychologist

Many beginning therapists (and some veterans) are drawn to self psychology because the techniques, initially at least, involve expressions of empathy and understanding rather than complex or obscure psychoanalytic formulations. One such case concerned a talented beginner, a particularly warm and empathic woman in her early thirties, who was treating a young woman along self psychological lines; to her consternation, empathy was not enough to achieve success with this patient.

The patient was a single, 32-year-old "starving artist" (actress) who had had negative experiences with seven previous therapists. She was a difficult patient who obviously had a need to find fault with her therapists, and she used words like "quack" or "hacker" or "total incompetent" to describe the therapists she had seen.

For two years this therapist attempted with her warmth and empathy and understanding and patience to melt down the patient's negative attitude. On the surface things seemed to be progressing nicely: the patient developed a self-object, idealizing transference and seemed to be making strides in her career and personal life. However, every four months the therapist sched-

uled a two-week vacation. These vacations were experienced by
the patient as complete empathic failures.

"You're just like all the others, just in it for the money," she
would complain prior to each vacation. "You can't wait to get
away from me, can you? If you want to know the truth, the truth
is that I think you don't care about anybody but yourself. You
have to have your vacation no matter what. I could be on the
verge of suicide, and you'd still take your idiotic vacation to
Greece or wherever the hell you're going. You're just another incompetent, uncaring, mercenary like all the rest."

The therapist attempted to listen understandingly, empathically, and patiently to such diatribes, and to the ones that followed her return from each vacation, lasting several sessions.
However, over time she found herself feeling more and more re-
sentful towards the patient. Here she was lavishing this patient
with warmth and understanding, and all she was getting back
was hostility. What was going wrong?

The therapist had had an unusually critical, perfectionistic
mother. Her countertransference had two aspects: on the one
hand, she had a profound need to be right, to be morally, ethically
correct; and on the other hand, she resented not being cared
about and loved just for who she was, right or wrong. Her
mother's love had always been conditional, and the therapist unconsciously still longed to be accepted and loved regardless of being right. She resented this patient because, like her mother, this
patient's positive feelings (her idealization) was based on condi-
tions: she was not to take vacations. Her resentment towards the
patient was both an expression of anger at her mother's conditional acceptance, and also of narcissistic rage about not being
loved because of imperfections.

By the end of the second year of therapy the therapist had
lost confidence in herself. She had tried to follow the precepts of
self psychology religiously, yet she was failing. The patient was
becoming more abusive and seemed on the verge of leaving. In
her therapy and supervision, the therapist came to understand,

gradually, her countertransference; the patient was making her feel incompetent and imperfect, just as her mother had done. Once she had extricated herself from this subjective counter-transference, she could once again be empathic toward the patient and begin to utilize other techniques in addition to those of self psychology—namely those involved with the analysis of the patient's transference and resistance. She had never wanted to upset her mother, and she never wanted to upset this patient—hence she had been reluctant to interpret. However, she finally said to the patient one day, "I'm sure that I'm not perfect, and that I have many faults, and that your criticism of me might be to some extent valid. But I also think it's important to note that you've found fault with all of your therapists, and you find fault with all your friends, and in fact throughout your life all your relationships have broken down because you began to feel critical of people."

"So? What are you trying to say? Are you saying that I'm a demanding, critical bitch? That's what my boyfriend says. Is that what you're saying now?" The patient was indeed upset by this interpretation and remained upset for many sessions; however, it was the turning point of the therapy, for it opened up an entirely new channel of communication. Utilizing her warmth and empathy, the therapist was able to gently guide the patient towards greater objectivity about herself.

Blunder 46

The Vain Therapist and the Slob

There was a therapist who was quite vain about his image. He always dressed fashionably, kept his clothes almost perfectly cleaned and pressed, had his hair cut and blow-dried once a week, and sat under a sunlamp or under the sun in the summer in order to maintain a tanned, healthy appearance. When confronted about his obsession with image, he would cite Freud's similar concerns, saying, "How one looks has a great impact on how one feels about oneself." This was, of course, a rationalization; at the bottom of this obsession was a childhood in which the therapist had been made to feel ugly by his parents; his mother had never wanted him and had given him inadequate mirroring from the beginning, while his father had been equally inadequate. Both teased him about his ears, which stuck out, and about his nose, which was too long, and about other aspects of his appearance. In order to compensate for what he thought to be an ugly body, he had taken early on to dressing well; this too was ridiculed by his parents, but he persisted even more strongly to emphasize his correctness of attire, and he also began disparaging the way his parents dressed, accusing them of being slobs.

Most of the therapist's patients were, like the therapist, narcissistic about their image. However, on one occasion a man came to see him who was quite disheveled, with unkempt hair, pale, pimpled skin, wrinkly clothes, and dirty fingernails. From the beginning the therapist could hardly restrain his disapproval of this patient's appearance, while, at the same time, the patient did not at all restrain his disapproval of the therapist. "Hey, what do you do anyway, sit under a sunlamp everyday? I mean, I think it's ridiculous to put so much into your appearance."

The patient, who was threatened by the neatness of the therapist's appearance (which called attention to his own slovenliness), began more and more to sound like the therapist's parents. By the third session, the therapist had had enough.

"Have you taken a good look at yourself? You think I'm *too neat*? Look at you. Your clothes look as though they've never been washed in your lifetime. Your hair looks like it's never been washed or combed. Your skin looks like the surface of the moon. I think maybe you could stand to look a bit more neat, don't you?" The therapist rattled on in this fashion a few more minutes, while the patient looked on with an ashen face. Finally the therapist caught himself, blushed, and said, "I'm sorry. Obviously you and I aren't suited for one another. I recommend you see another therapist."

The patient was only too happy to agree, and the session ended abruptly at that point.

Blunder 47

The Therapist Who Meddled

After having a six-year affair with her employer, the dream of an attractive woman in her forties seemed about to be fulfilled. The employer had left his wife, she had left her husband, and the two of them had moved in with one another. The next step, after their divorces became final, was for them to get married. For a while she was in ecstasy.

Then the employer began exhibiting at home the same autocratic behavior he had displayed at the office. He ordered the woman to do this and to do that and was insensitive to her feelings. The couple began having arguments, and the woman sought out a therapist for advice.

The therapist she ended up with was a rather assertive woman who had recently divorced her husband—whom she saw as weak and ineffectual—and now supported herself and her children by doing therapy. Her own mother had been the dominant figure in the household, and the therapist had strong feelings about women being assertive towards men. This need to be dominant was in part a defense against the narcissistic rage connected with feelings of inferiority about being female. This narcissistic rage caused her to pick ineffectual men such as her ex-husband, whom she could dominate, and then when she did so she had contempt for them and left them. Her unconscious need was to prove that she was superior to men.

Naturally she was appalled by this patient's description of her employer–lover. She would certainly never take that kind of "bossing" from any man. However, she was professional enough not to make any direct judgments about the patient's would-be spouse; instead, she made subtle suggestions as to how the patient was to behave towards her mate. In essence, she encouraged the patient to be assertive in the manner that she and her mother were assertive with men. The patient took the therapist's suggestions, but instead of improving their relationship, the therapist's interventions aggravated the situation so much that the couple was on the brink of breaking up–which, unconsciously, was what the therapist wanted.

The therapist brought the case to the attention of her supervisor, and he pointed out to her that she was acting out a narcissistic countertransference identification with her patient; she was failing to distinguish the difference between herself and her patient, failing to view the patient on her own terms. The therapist had a need to be assertive, even dominating; the patient did not. The patient was basically comfortable with allowing her husband-to-be to "wear the pants," that is, she was comfortable being the submissive partner in the relationship and did not want to change that. In addition, she was not particularly introspective and did not have the aptitude for–nor had she sought out–a reconstructive type of therapy experience. She had wanted counselling. She was basically happy with her mate; both had left their spouses for each other and had made a commitment. To attempt to radically change her and her relationship with him would only lead to the possible destruction of what was clearly a preference for both of them.

Once she had taken in her supervisor's interpretation, she was able to give the patient what she wanted and needed–advice on how to resolve problems with her husband that was empathic to the patient's own objectives and philosophy. On the therapist's advice, the patient quit her job in order to devote herself to being a wife and mother; this eliminated some of the friction, which was due to seeing too much of her husband (day and night) and attempting to wear too many hats. In addition, the therapist advised her to gently assert herself in small, nonconfrontational ways, and the husband gradually toned down his bossiness – that is, he learned to be the head of the household without being tyrannical about it. After a few months the patient felt her goals had been obtained, and the therapy was successfully terminated.

Blunder 48

The Primal Therapist

The therapeutic community of a large city was shocked when one of its members, a leading practitioner of primal therapy, died suddenly of a stroke at the age of 37. One of his therapist acquaintances said in private that he had died of "an overdose of screams."

For over fourteen years this therapist had practiced primal therapy, averaging about thirty-five hours a week, with time off during summers and Christmas. He saw each patient for two-hour sessions, and for most of these sessions the patient was encouraged to cry or scream out long repressed infantile feelings. Such screams are generally ear-splitting, so the therapist had taken to wearing earplugs during working hours. However, he neglected to understand the long-term effect of such work on his emotions. In order to be with somebody who is screaming, a therapist must suppress his or her emotions. This kind of chronic suppression of an impulse to emote (screaming is contagious) can lead, over the years, to a stroke. In the case of this therapist, he was constantly constricting the veins in his temples in order to suppress his own feelings and immunize himself against his response to his patient's screams. He had constant headaches. Yet, all of this happened gradually without his paying attention to it happening. The stroke was as much a surprise to him as to anybody else.

In fact, his own characterological structure caused him to be blind to what he was doing to himself. He himself was quite repressed and had a lot of unconscious infantile rage; however, he had been the son of a Methodist minister and had been drilled by his father on good and evil—namely, that any person who harbored anger, rage, or hatred of another person was the Devil incarnate. The therapist therefore had a mission to help other people exorcise their evil spirits through primal therapy. By helping others he could vicariously help himself, or so he unconsciously thought.

This is an example of a narcissistic countertransference; each patient becomes an extension of the self. However, such therapists often do both themselves and their patients a disservice. While they are able to help patients to work through early infantile material, they neglect completely the analysis of the transference, an understanding of which is important in helping the patient learn what it is that impedes his relationships. They often neglect their own emotional states, too, sometimes with disastrous consequences.

Blunder 49

The Therapist Who Needed a Self-Object

"Oh, God, my life is such a mess. I don't know if I'll ever feel happy again," a young, attractive woman with reddish hair and sparkling green eyes murmured to her therapist. She sat forlornly in her chair, rocking slightly to and fro, sighing. "Everything seems so hopeless."

"Things will get better soon. Believe me," the therapist, an older man, replied compassionately.

In the early stages of therapy this patient was very needy, had extremely low self-esteem, and needed a great deal of support and affirmation. The therapist gave her that support and affirmation and was indeed very helpful to her. She made major strides in her professional, social, sexual, and family relationships, and she was grateful to the therapist and idealized him, making him into a "good daddy." However, after the initial phase had ended and the middle phase of therapy had begun, the patient's characterological problems began to surface. She stopped paying her bills, used her flattery in a manipulative way, and was very seductive, also as a manipulation.

The therapist succumbed to her manipulations not because he entertained any inappropriate sexual intentions toward her, but because he enjoyed her praise and her idealization of him. His mother had been rejecting and depriving, and he had a need for narcissistic reflection. The patient provided him with the adulation he had never gotten from his mother. She became a perfect self-object, one that helped him to like himself better. The patient's idealization was so gratifying for him, in fact, that he never confronted her about her manipulative behavior or her financial exploitation, nor did he confront her about the fact that she had exhibited similar behavior with men she had gone out with.

After a while the therapist began to feel angry at the patient without knowing why. Then he began to feel a rage, as it began to dawn on him that the patient had stopped idealizing him and was treating him with contempt. This came to light during a session when she began to laugh at something he had said.

"What's the laughter about?" he asked.

"I just thought what you said was funny."

"It sounded more like you were laughing at me."

"I wasn't really laughing at you," she said at first. Then she laughed again, holding her hand over her mouth like a devilish child. "Well, I guess I am laughing at you. You're, well, amusing at times. You try so hard to say the proper thing, and then it comes out wrong anyway. It's cute." She smirked at the therapist, and he went pale.

"I see." He glared at her. "You think I'm cute? It sounds as though you don't have very much respect for me."

She denied this emphatically. "Oh, no, that's not true. I was just laughing. Don't take it personally."

"I'm not taking it personally," the therapist lied. "I just find it interesting that you don't seem to have very much respect for me anymore, and I'm wondering how that came about."

"You're *so* serious sometimes," she said, making a seductive, green-eyed face at him. And she began laughing again.

By this time the therapist had become so enraged he could not meaningfully confront the patient and analyze her resistant behavior. She left the session feeling uneasy about the interchange, and she did not return for the following appointment. The therapist ended up losing the patient, a great deal of money, and some of his self-respect.

Blunder 50

The Therapist Who
Needed To Be the World's Greatest Authority

A young woman patient whose life was a disaster both personally and professionally went into treatment with a well-known authority—a therapist who was an author, a lecturer, and a teacher who had made frequent appearances on television. The young woman quickly became a "groupie" of this therapist.

As long as the patient was riddled with anxiety and helplessness, and she put herself completely in the hands of the therapist, the relationship was a productive one. The patient had a need to idealize the therapist (to recreate in the therapy relationship the omniscient "good" mother she had lost in early infancy), and the therapist had a need to be idealized. The patient took the therapist as her role model and, over the course of the years, became a therapist herself. In fact, the therapist's interpretations and advice with respect to the patient's professional life had been quite effective.

However, she was not able to be helpful in helping the patient with her personal life, because the therapist's own personal life was fraught with difficulties. She was one of these "public personalities" who sublimate everything into their professions and have no real personal life. Up to a certain point the patient did not allow herself to become aware of her therapist's personal inadequacies; however, as her ego strength increased, she began to look at the therapist more objectively – she deidealized her; she started questioning some of the therapist's views and methods.

"I don't think you know what you're saying," the therapist replied. "I think maybe you're starting to feel competitive with me and threatened by me," she added. Her manner and her words seemed to be saying to her patient, "Who do you think you are, challenging a world-renowned authority like me?"

However, the patient became more and more resistant, and she questioned the therapist's methods more and more. Finally, the therapist became enraged and kicked the patient out of therapy.

"If you can't follow my advice, I don't want you as a patient," she told her. "It's a waste of your time and mine."

Rather than perceiving the patient's opposition to her as a healthy attempt at separation and deidealization, this narcissistic therapist – who in fact had a need to be "the world's greatest authority" in order to ward off feelings of personal inadequacy the patient had threatened to arouse – was wounded by being deidealized by her former "groupie." Her narcissistic rage was rekindled, the rage that she had first felt when she was treated by her mother, in her infancy and early childhood, as though she were worthless and told repeatedly that she would never amount to anything. Thus she dismissed the patient in a manner that was traumatic to the patient. The latter was so traumatized by this experience that it took her several years before she was able to reenter therapy, with another therapist, and continue to work out her personal problems.

Blunder 51

The Patient Who Took a Vacation

A male patient decided to take a vacation to South America for two months; when he imparted this decision to his therapist, he had a smile of triumph on his face. He experienced his decision to take a vacation as a victory over the therapist both because he would then free himself from the therapist (who represented his projected harsh superego) and because he could afford the trip and the therapist could not.

The therapist became irritated by this abandonment and jealous of the patient's wealth. However, he pushed these feelings aside and responded, "That's nice. Where will you go?" The patient gave him a full itinerary, and the two pretended that everything was fine. The therapist was too angry at the patient to analyze his behavior; so he pretended to be happy for the patient, in this way also depriving him of the fruits of his victory (his anger).

However, in the sessions remaining before the scheduled vacation, the patient began feeling anxious that the therapist would seek revenge for the patient's triumph. In anticipation of this aggression by the therapist, he became ill with a virus and eventually had to cancel his trip. The therapist took pleasure in this cancellation at first, feeling that the patient had automatically come to his senses. Then he began to feel anxious.

After talking the matter over with his supervisor he understood the source of his anxiety. He felt guilty about taking satisfaction in the patient's illness and realized that he felt responsible for it. By withholding not only his anger at the patient, but also his interpretation, he was subtly inducing guilt in the patient (utilizing the same method his mother had used with him as a boy).

At the next session the therapist interpreted the entire interaction for the patient, and the patient understood and agreed; the therapy was back on course once again.

Blunder 52

The Negative Therapeutic Reaction

There was a young female patient of the type that is the bane of many a young therapist (and a goodly number of experienced ones as well): she was a chronic complainer. Her "number" was to prove that she was a hapless victim and that nothing good could possibly befall her. She specialized in the "yes, but . . ." routine.

Patient: "My life would really be different if I dyed my hair blonde. Then I know men would be attracted to me."

Therapist: "Wonderful. Why don't you dye your hair blonde?"

Patient: "Yes, but then I would lose my natural look and attitude. I wouldn't be authentic anymore. No, what I really need to do is to leave this shitty, stupid job. I hate this job. It demeans me. I can't use my talent or creativity in it at all. God, I hate it."

Therapist: "Terrific. I agree. You really ought to change jobs."

Patient: "Yes, but with my luck, I'd never find another job. I don't know, if I could just meet the right man. . . ."

Therapist: "That's an idea. Maybe you should go out more, try to meet somebody."

Patient: "Yes, but the men I meet always turn out to be either nerds or jerks. I don't know what to do."

Therapist: (Thinks to herself) Go to hell!

The patient was a classic case of negative therapeutic reaction. She had a greater stake in being a victim than in getting better. She had so much rage against her mother (who prodded her to be a success) that she got more mileage out of failing and frustrating her mother than she would have by succeeding. Meanwhile, the therapist had had a mother who was, like this patient, a complainer and who would never accept help. The therapist had spent a lifetime attempting to make her mother happy. She was trying to heal a narcissistic wound by pulling off this magic act first with her mother and now with this patient. With the patient she had taken a Kohutian stance of empathy and support, sans interpretation. She was going to be such a warm, understanding therapist that she would melt even this heart of stone. She had done the same thing in her personal relationships, being always drawn to "bad guys" who she aspired to turn into "good guys" through her love. It didn't work in her personal life, and it didn't work with this patient.

The therapist grew angrier and angrier at the patient, but said nothing. Finally came the coup-de-grace: the patient told the therapist that the therapy wasn't going anywhere, that she was feeling worse instead of better. "I think I need to see a psychiatrist as a consultant. Please don't take it personally, but I don't know if you're experienced enough for me. I don't know. Maybe I need medication. Anyway, it's worth a try."

The therapist was, actually, delighted. At that point she was so frustrated that it had become a case of "take my patient, please!"

The psychiatrist she referred the patient to was also an experienced psychoanalyst. He gave the patient a prescription, but told the therapist he did not really feel it would help. He also explained to the therapist that the patient was involved in a negative therapeutic reaction and correctly predicted she would never

take the medicine. He was right; she took a few pills and complained that it made her feel worse.

Finally, with the psychiatrist's feedback to bolster her, the
therapist began confronting the patient's character resistance,
and the therapy started to move forward.

The Chip off the Old Block

There was a therapist who was very disappointed in his son. The therapist, who was of middle age, had wanted his son to be "a chip off the old block"–that is, to follow him into his profession. Instead, the son chose an altogether different field and was a failure at that one.

One day the therapist took on a new patient–an extraordinarily bright young man who was a graduate student in psychology and on the path to becoming a therapist–and the therapist's spirits began to lift. It was "love at first sight." This patient's father was also a therapist, but an unsuccessful one, and the patient was disappointed in his father not only professionally but also because of his father's lack of warmth toward him and lack of appreciation for his talents. The patient found the father he always wanted, and the therapist found the son he longed for. This combination was obvious to both of them and might have fostered an ideal working alliance.

Instead, a collusion developed. The therapist's unconscious and not-so-unconscious agenda began to be oppressive to the patient. He was being groomed by the therapist as a narcissistic extension; he would be the heir-apparent who would carry on with the therapist's work and interests. The two talked too much about the field and veered away from focusing on the patient's psychological issues. And, most important, the patient began withholding material and evading issues, particularly negative transference reactions. The therapist, in the service of promoting his own dream, was selectively inattentive (counterresistant) to material that he would otherwise have noticed.

Eventually the young patient came in and announced, "I've found another therapist. I've found that I've become increasingly uncomfortable with you; in fact, I find you to be oppressive, and I feel very angry at you for oppressing me. I feel really disappointed that you have let things go on in this way." The therapist, shocked and heartbroken, asked if the patient wanted to continue a personal relationship. The patient said he did not.

The therapist had unwittingly become, transferentially, the patient's disappointing father, and instead of discovering a new way of dealing with a "son," which would have produced a healthy relationship, he had repeated the same pattern that had alienated him from his own son.

Blunder 54

The Contemptuous Therapist

A male patient could not get much sympathy from his female therapist when he began an affair with a younger woman. He saw his wife as a castrating, demanding figure like his mother, and saw his affair with the younger woman, who was very supportive to him, as healthy. However, his therapist did not view the situation in the same way. Though she never came out and said it directly, she felt sympathetic to the patient's wife, while perceiving the patient's affair with the younger woman as an act of spite and immaturity, not to mention betrayal.

The patient, sensing the therapist's censure, repeatedly asked her, "Do you think I'm doing the right thing?"

"Only you can answer that," she would reply. "Since you're asking that question, perhaps you have some doubts."

"Of course. I have plenty of doubts. I've never had an affair before in my fourteen years of marriage. I feel confused. I feel scared. But I love Jenny so much, and she loves me."

"And what about Ellen? What do you feel for her? And what do you think she's feeling?"

Again and again the therapist would attempt to direct the man's attention on how he was treating his wife. He would always change the subject at such times, feeling as though he were on a witness stand instead of in a therapy office.

The therapist was herself an older woman whose husband had left her for a younger woman. In addition, her father had once had an affair with his secretary, which caused her and her mother much consternation. Meanwhile, her mother was a self-righteous, martyr type who had, unconsciously, driven her husband to this affair through her coldness and fear of sex; this coldness (hatred of men) and the fear of sex had also been transmitted to her daughter, who had driven her husband to divorce her for a younger woman. Neither mother nor daughter had been able to take responsibility for their contribution to their failed relationships; instead, they both blamed their husbands and used these instances as justifications for their anger at men. The therapist had not completely analyzed these issues; hence, there was a failure of empathy toward this particular patient. She unconsciously responded to his dilemma as though he were her ex-husband or her father. In effect, she behaved in a way so as to express her unconscious contempt, an outgrowth of her narcissistic rage at her father, her mother, and at men, all of which served to antagonize the patient.

"I don't feel I'm getting much sympathy from you," the patient complained over and over.

And the therapist was repeatedly surprised by such statements. "Of course I sympathize with you," she would respond, thereby cutting off any further exploration of the subject.

Sometimes the patient would persist anyway. "But I *feel* you're judging me."

"That's ridiculous. Anytime I say anything to you that opposes what you want to hear, you feel I'm judging you."

No matter what the patient said, she always managed to turn it back on him or deride him. He finally stopped talking about much of anything during his sessions, and, after several more months at an impasse, he told her he had decided to leave for a more sympathetic therapist.

"You mean you want to see a therapist who will 'yes' everything you say, right?"

Even upon terminating, the patient's attempt to communicate his frustration to the therapist was met with derision. The patient left feeling angry, defeated, and inadequate. The therapist had managed, at the patient's expense, to maintain her narcissistic self-righteous image intact.

Blunder 55

The Therapist Who Feared Abandonment

There was a young female therapist who continually feared that all her patients were going to leave her. In particular, she feared that her women patients were going to leave her. The therapist's own mother had walked out of her life when she was 4 years old and had gone off to live in a foreign land, never to be heard from again. In her countertransference relationships with her female patients, they became her mother and she the dutiful daughter who, this time around, would so please and console them that they would be too contented and grateful to leave. However, to her consternation, no matter how wonderful she was to her patients, many of them left her anyway. In fact, the nicer she was to them, the more critical they became of her, and the sooner they left.

For instance, she had one patient, an older woman who had come to her complaining about problems in her marriage, who used to begin each session with the statement, "I didn't want to come here today."

Immediately the therapist began to dread the next sentence, because she always thought it was going to be, "So I've decided to quit therapy."

However, usually the patient went on to say she didn't want

to come in because it meant facing up to her problems with her husband.

After several months of this, the patient began to pick up, unconsciously, the therapist's fear of losing her, and the patient became contemptuous of the therapist. Soon she was saying that she didn't think the therapist was helping her. Then she was saying she didn't think the therapist was smart enough for her, experienced enough, old enough. The patient became more and more critical as a way of defending against her anxiety about being in therapy, and the therapist attempted to remain neutral, usually responding with, "How do you want me to help you? What would it mean if I were smarter, more experienced, older? What would be different?" These responses seemed only momentarily to quell the patient's contempt.

Finally a day came when the therapist could take it no more. There was another burst of criticism by the patient in which she speculated that the therapist was quite wrong for her, temperamentally. The therapist sighed and retorted in a nervous voice, "You know, perhaps I'm not the right therapist for you. Perhaps it would be best if you found another therapist more suitable to you."

"I was thinking the same thing," the patient hastily replied, glad to have the therapist take responsibility for the termination. A week later she called to say she had found another therapist.

Sometimes "nice" therapists finish last.

Blunder 56

The Critical Mother

A female therapist with fifteen years' experience but no doctorate was seeing a very volatile, provocative, borderline patient. At
one point in her therapy the patient, with great difficulty, managed to obtain a doctorate in a scientific subject. The patient now
used this to attack the therapist for being remiss in not obtaining
a doctorate of her own, for not having sufficient academic training
to be an adequate therapist, for failing her and depriving her.

"This is ridiculous," the patient would say. "When are you going to get your doctorate? Here I'm your patient, and I have a doctorate and you don't."

"What would it mean to you if I had a doctorate?" the therapist replied.

"It would mean you'd be able to help me more. By not having
a doctorate you're depriving me of my one chance for mental
health. I mean it. It's ridiculous. All my friends' therapists have
doctorates. Why won't you apply to Columbia? New York Uni-
versity? And don't tell me you don't have the money, because you
could take out a student loan."

The therapist herself had had many misgivings about her
lack of academic credentials, misgivings that were substantiated

by state licensing authorities, insurance companies, and some of her colleagues. Nevertheless, the therapist had had excellent training, had been fairly well psychoanalyzed, and had been a successful and effective practitioner for many years. Essentially this was a clash between a patient who had been deprived by her mother (inadequate mothering) and a therapist who had had a critical and verbally abusive mother, one who constantly derogated her. Therefore, whenever the patient went off on one of her critical barrages, the therapist became anxious. She was skilled and experienced enough not to commit any gross blunder such as defending herself or attacking the patient. However, the best she could come up with was to suggest that the patient find another therapist.

"If I'm depriving you the way you say I am," the therapist told her, "then perhaps you should seek out another therapist, one who has the academic credentials you desire."

"Maybe I'll do that," the patient retorted.

They went on and on about this for another few months. The therapist's anxiety grew. This anxiety was due to a revival of her own rage toward her critical mother. She began more and more to see her patient as a critical mother and to want to annihilate her. Fearful that this rage would erupt and get out of control, the therapist kept pushing for termination, and eventually helped the patient find another therapist.

"You will be pleased with this woman," the therapist said. "And she's not only a very good therapist, but also has a doctorate from a good school. Give her a try, and if she doesn't work out I'll be glad to give you another referral."

A proper therapeutic response would have been for the therapist to be empathic to the patient's anger at having been deprived of "good enough mothering," to provide a holding environment that was missing in the patient's childhood, and allow her to work through the negative feelings so she could get in touch with the longing underneath.

Blunder 57

The Therapist Who
Financially Exploited His Patient

The patient was an exceptionally bright and handsome man in his early forties who had been reasonably successful in his own field when he began therapy with a well-known therapist. The therapist induced him to give up his own work and start seeing patients under the therapist's auspices and supervision, while simultaneously continuing his therapy. The patient was a homosexual who had been totally rejected by his blue-collar father; now he had seemingly found a father who appreciated him and would apprentice him in his own field. He was naturally elated at this prospect.

However, the patient had had absolutely no training in therapy, not even a college course in psychology.

"How in the world," he asked his analyst, "am I going to do therapy? I don't know what I'm doing. I don't know anything about emotional problems."

"Don't worry," the therapist replied. "I'll do the intakes, make the diagnoses and treatment plan, and supervise your therapy very closely."

The patient was dubious and terrified at the thought of treating patients without any training; however, "father knows best." He gave up his occupation and was given a small office in his therapist's building. Since the therapist was well known, he had a plethora of patients to refer. They came in droves, often without an intake or treatment plan, and the promised supervision was reduced to three or four sentences at the end of the patient's paid-for therapy sessions. The patient sometimes made as much as $1000 a week for his mentor and was given a stipend of $150 a week. Fortunately, the patient was such an intelligent, warm, intuitive person and had such a presence of mind and integrity that even without training he probably did his patients more good and less harm than his mentor. However, because he had such integrity, he felt terribly guilty. He also realized that he was ensconced in a career for which he had absolutely no credentials, was totally dependent upon his therapist for referrals, and would have no means of support without him. This made him frightened of crossing his therapist and not complying with all of his requests.

Eventually, though, he began to feel more and more anger at being exploited; he approached his mentor with a request for a higher stipend, accompanying this request with a mild threat to quit.

"Don't threaten me," the therapist responded. "If you make any trouble for me I'll prosecute *you* for practicing illegally."

The patient became confused, angry, depressed, and anxious; at this point he went to another therapist. Eventually he was able, with some difficulty, to leave his old therapist, but he was left with a shattered sense of self as well as a shattered life. He was no longer able to pursue his original career, and he felt he could not in good conscience continue to do therapy. Luckily he had found another male therapist who really *was* a good father to him, and he was able to overcome the damage done to him during his six years with the previous therapist.

The therapist in this case was acting out feelings of narcissistic omniscience while, at the same time, defending against the negative oedipal complex. Consciously he felt he was really helping this patient by taking him under his wing and providing him with this new occupation. He felt the patient was ideally suited to be a therapist and that it would be therapeutic for him to experience himself helping others. To an extent it was. However, unconsciously this therapist was making the patient a narcissistic extension of himself, molding him in his own image, without regard to what the patient really wanted. He was also contemptuous of the patient, unconsciously, for being a homosexual, and warded off his own latent homosexuality by exploiting the patient's need for a good father who would accept him as a man. In thus acting contemptuously toward the patient, he was denying his own homosexual urges, projecting them onto the patient and demeaning them; hence his own self-hatred was directed externally at the patient.

Unfortunately the therapist's narcissistic, sadistic, and psychopathic character traits were so ego-syntonic that no supervision or training analysis had been able to reach him.

Blunder 58

The Incomplete Interpretation

During one of his sessions with a very educated, refined female therapist, a young male patient spoke disparagingly of his relationships with women.

"I feel so frustrated. I can't tell you how frustrated I feel. Frustrated and angry. I just can't seem to ever get anywhere with the kinds of women I'm attracted to."

"What kinds of women are you attracted to?" the therapist asked.

"I'm attracted to women who're, I don't know. . . . I guess what I'm trying to say is I'm attracted to women who I see as superior to me—women who are refined and independent and smart. But I always get rejected by them. They always turn out to be snots, nasty bitches, who get a kick out of rejecting me and making me feel bad about myself. Then I feel frustrated and angry, and I want to do something to them—you know, reject them, torture them, humiliate them. Sometimes, well, sometimes I've even fantasized about rubbing shit in their faces. I guess you think that's awful. What do you think of all this?"

The therapist paused, then gave her interpretation. "I think when you're talking about your frustration and anger at refined

and independent and smart women, you desire to torture or humiliate them, you're really talking about me. You're transferring
your frustrating and rejecting mother onto me, and you're telling
me that you're angry at me and that you want to torture me because you think I'm going to reject and torture you. In a way, I
think you're warning me that you might destroy me because of
what I represent to you."

The patient listened to the interpretation and seemed to
take it in; however, for the remainder of the session he became
depressed, morose, and for several sessions afterward he remained the same. Why the depression? Why the withdrawal?

The therapist had given a correct but incomplete interpretation. The patient needed and was seeking something through his
complaints to the therapist about the women in his life—he was
seeking to connect himself with an object emotionally and
libidinally, as the previous sessions had awakened his feelings of
tenderness and love for the therapist. His complaints were an attempt to fend off his new, but threatening, feelings of tenderness.
Indirectly he was asking the therapist if he could really trust her,
if he could really let down his guard with her, if he could surren-
der without running the risk of suffering the humiliations he had
always suffered before. The therapist had been unable to give the
patient this part of the interpretation because of her own narcissistic countertransference. She had related only to his anger and
his debasing tendencies toward women and had felt, through an
identification with women in general, narcissistically wounded by
the patient's complaints about "snotty, bitchy women." She had
not been able to be empathic and receptive to his tender, vulnerable feelings. Her incomplete interpretation had focused only on
the negative, which only succeeded in alienating the patient.

Blunder 59

The Pregnant Therapist

When a therapist became pregnant, a certain male patient began to express disapproval of her state.

"Aren't you a little too old to have a baby?" he asked at one point, when pressed by her. And at another point he said, "Frankly, I think women look dumpy when they're pregnant." And, at yet another point he said, "I should think you'd want to devote yourself to your career, to helping your patients, and not to having babies."

On a conscious level the therapist could understand where the patient was coming from. When he was 3 years old, his mother had become pregnant and had made a big effort to prepare the patient for the arrival of a younger sibling. His mother had read some popular psychology books that had advised doing this, but she had carried it too far, to a point where the patient had wanted to say, "All right, enough!" Deep down he began more and more to resent his mother being pregnant, and he saw her as ugly (his anger at her affecting his perception of her). Then, when the baby arrived it was a girl—which the mother had always wanted—and the baby received much more attention from the mother than the patient ever had. Now he was transferring the pregnant, rejecting image of his mother onto his therapist.

The therapist understood this, but unconsciously she resented the patient for disparaging her. She felt narcissistically wounded by him. The patient represented her own projected superego, which similarly took a disparaging view of motherhood. Her own ideal image of herself was not as a mother, but as a strong, independent career woman, and she had deep conflicts around the issue of career versus motherhood that had caused her to delay the matter until her late thirties. This conflict, on a deeper plane, had to do with her conflicts about being female and about her femininity in particular. In her family milieu, traditionally masculine virtues were extolled and traditionally feminine qualities were demeaned. Hence the patient's negative attitude towards her pregnancy was a recreation of experiences she had undergone in her childhood. Feelings of inferiority about her femininity were revived, and the narcissistic wound surrounding these conflicts was reopened.

As a result, the therapist found herself being defensive with the patient about her pregnancy. "I happen to think pregnant women are beautiful," she said at one point. And at another point she asked him a bit too bluntly, "Perhaps my pregnancy reminds you of your situation with your mother. Did you ever think of that?"

Of course the patient had thought of that, but the way in which the therapist brought it to his attention now made him want to ignore her and keep on pressing his attack of her.

The therapy relationship remained at a stalemate throughout the pregnancy, and it was only afterwards that the two were able to get beyond their defensive postures and resume their quest for the truth.

Blunder 60

The Therapist Who Felt Snubbed by a Psychotic

He was a young therapist working in a mental hospital who had grown attached to a beautiful young patient. The patient was not only beautiful but gave off an aura of supreme wisdom and confidence. There was always about her a knowing smile, a proud gait, a telling wrinkle of the brow. It was as though, in looking at somebody with her light blue eyes, she could see to the core of his or her being. Such was the case whenever the therapist "came to call on her," as she would put it. She would gaze at him in her knowing way, and he felt *known*.

There are some psychotic patients who are brilliantly psychotic, who can convince nearly everybody that the delusions they harbor about themselves and the world are real. This woman's delusion was that she was omniscient. She would not come right out and say so; instead, it was implied indirectly through what she said and how she behaved. She tended to speak cryptically, as many psychotics do – a defense she needed in order to survive in a hostile family milieu. When she spoke in this wise, calm cryptic manner, looking into the therapist's eyes with a knowing wrinkle in her brows, the therapist could not help but think there must be some truth to what she was saying. So he listened to her with a great deal of respect and, yes, even admiration, this despite the fact that when she wasn't in session with him she was prone to painting dark, smoldering portraits of ghoulish people on the walls of her room, sometimes using her own feces to accentuate certain features, and in other ways acting out a discordant rage that seemed to belie her delusion of calm wisdom.

The young man had a narcissistic need to merge with an omniscient mother figure, stemming from a fixation at the oral stage that he had not as yet completely worked through in his own therapy. Hence he continued more and more to be enraptured by this patient.

However, more and more the patient began to lose interest in the therapy and in the therapist. She would come late to the sessions and speak even more cryptically, so that he could not make sense of what she was saying. Then she began being more and more critical of him, and even throw up her hands and laugh at him. "There are some things you can't know," she responded when he persisted in trying to make sense of what she was saying. "There are some things you're not ready to know."

"When will I be ready?"

"When you're ready."

"When is that."

"You'll know when it's time."

"I will."

"Yes . . . you will."

A knowing smirk.

The therapist grew angry at her. He felt snubbed by her. Consciously he realized that she was a woman with severe problems; but unconsciously he had developed countertransference feelings towards her. Without his knowing it, she had become his long sought after omniscient mother, who through her acceptance would make him whole again. However, she had not accepted him; she, like his mother, had found him unworthy of her inner world and had shut him out. So convincing was her delusional system and so strong was his susceptibility to it that despite his professional training he was completely taken in by it.

When the patient did not come in for the next few sessions, he expressed his rage about her to his supervisor. Both he and his supervisor realized that he was far too caught up in the swirl to continue with her, and he was removed from the case. He was not the first therapist to suffer that fate with this particular patient, nor the last.

Blunder 61

The Grandiose Therapist
and the Seductive, Submissive Patient

A novice male therapist had not resolved his need to be special, rooted in his relationship with his mother which, in the earliest days, consisted of his mother treating him as though he were indeed the most special creature on the planet. That relationship with his mother, however, was cut short when she suddenly died of cancer. Thereafter his father and his stepmother did not treat him as though he were special at all; in fact, they treated him as though he was a demanding, spoiled child, and they ridiculed him. As an adult he still had a need to be treated specially, and this flaw in his character often got in the way of his doing therapy.

A very attractive, borderline young woman came to see him, complaining of sexual abuse by her older brother when she was a child and of her current relationships with men, none of which satisfied her, none of which she could trust. "I usually end up rejecting them," she said. "In fact, I'm always the one who breaks it off, usually quite suddenly." The therapist did not pay proper attention to these warnings, because he found himself attracted to the young woman. He was attracted to her because from the beginning she related to him in a submissive, seductive manner.

She would call him by his title, "Dr._____," several times

each session, would usually smile upwardly at him, as though looking up at a god, bowing her head slightly, and she was always apologizing and depreciating herself before him and treating him in every way with the highest respect and admiration. While remaining overtly guarded, unconsciously the therapist "sucked at the breast" of this "fairy godmother," who had recognized how special a therapist he was. One day the patient brought in a dream.

> I dreamed we were in your office – you, me, and my boyfriend – and we were all in love with each other and everything and we all wanted to have sex. I felt as though I was in love with my boyfriend and I was also in love with you, and you were in love with me, but the two of us knew we would never have sex because my first loyalty was to my boyfriend. But knowing you were in love with me made me be able to trust you enough to do the therapy. . . .

The therapist felt more than a twinge of anxiety when he heard this dream, but he did not pay proper attention to this feeling. Once again, another part of him, his narcissistic grandiosity, "sucked at the breast" and felt flattered at this offer of intimacy.

Although he had studied borderline patients and knew the theories about submission – how it is always a defense against the desire to dominate, a form of appeasement designed to control both the therapist's and the patient's own aggressiveness – he did not give much thought to it in this instance. He was lulled, seduced, hypnotized because of his countertransference need to be idolized. He talked the patient into coming twice a week and she agreed, and he began thinking about her between sessions, thinking about how sweet a patient she was, wondering why all patients could not be as sweet and adoring and cooperative as she. At Christmas she gave him a special ornament she had made herself, saying she wanted him to think of her during the holidays. He did think of her during the holidays, and after.

Then one session she came in and mentioned flippantly that she was cutting back from twice a week to once a week. She mentioned it in passing, as though it were not of any importance, and went on to discuss some problems she was having with her boyfriend.

The therapist felt furious. "That's it? You've decided to cut down to once a week, just like that?"

"Yes. Why?" The patient looked at him with surprise.

"Don't you feel this is something that should be discussed with me?"

"Why should I discuss it with you? I'm the one who's paying for it. It's my therapy. Am I your prisoner or something?" The patient's entire manner had suddenly changed. Gone completely was her submissiveness. Instead she spoke to him in a contemptuous, flippant way. "What, do I have to ask your approval for everything I do? Are you my father or something?"

"I just thought it might be nice if you had included me in the decision," the therapist blurted out.

"Well, I'm sorry if you're feelings are hurt. But I have to do what I feel is best for me."

She had hit the nail on the head; his feelings were hurt, and he lapsed into silence for the rest of the session. By the end of the session he had become enraged at the thought that she had betrayed him—she had seduced him into loving her and now was abandoning him (as his mother had done)—and he acted out the rage by interrupting her in mid-sentence and informing her coldly that her time was up.

All week he had fantasies of terminating her in a vicious, nasty way. Had he been on top of these countertransference feelings, he might have guessed that this was precisely how the patient was feeling towards him, that *she* wanted to terminate him, partly to act out feelings of resentment that had built up inside her due to the fact that she had to be so submissive towards him, and partly in defense of some real, tender, longing feelings that were surfacing at that point. He was *not* on top of his feelings, and hence he was totally unprepared for what was to happen in the next session.

She came in bristling, telling him right off that she was quitting because she could not trust him after the previous session. "You were angry at me, and you weren't admitting it. You just cut me off at the end of the session like I was a piece of dirt. You know how sensitive I am about being cut off, but you did it anyway. I can't stay in therapy with you now. I'm quitting and that's that. Do you have anything to say?" She glared at him. Again, there was no sign of her former submissiveness; she had done a complete flipflop. She was now rejecting the therapist, just as she had rejected every other man in her life. And, because he was in the throes of his countertransference rage, he could not think of anything to say.

"No, I have nothing to say," he told her, hiding his rage behind a facade of calmness. "If you want to quit, there's the door."

She walked out smiling triumphantly. He spent several days agonizing over her, having fantasies of destroying her in different ways. After a week he called her and asked her to come in for a termination session, and she agreed to do so. However, at this session the therapist was still too enraged to be objective, and everything he said to her seemed like an accusation and an attack. He told her she was acting out her angry feelings about her older brother, that she wasn't doing herself any good, and that she should think it over. She agreed to think it over, but in reality her mind was made up and she had merely come in to appease him. She was too frightened of him now to continue with him, too frightened that he would at some point retaliate. She called him a day later to say she was still quitting and had decided to see a woman therapist. The therapist wished her good luck.

Then, as a last dig, she asked him, "I was wondering, are you still in therapy yourself?"

The therapist laughed somewhat bitterly. "No, dear, I'm not in therapy."

In a few days he called his old therapist. "Virginia, remember my little problem about needing women to treat me specially? The one I thought I'd licked? I think I need to talk to you about it some more."

PART TWO

FORTY COUNTERRESISTANCE BLUNDERS

Introduction

The following forty case histories are concerned with instances in which therapists resist various aspects of the process of therapy and by doing so impede therapeutic progress. Often, their resistances are induced by resistances of their patients; at other times their resistances spring entirely from within themselves—as when a therapist resists a patient's expressions of vulnerability and longing because he or she has not resolved those very same feelings of vulnerability and longing and wishes to deny their existence. Sometimes these resistances are largely characterological, having their roots in the therapist's complexes and fixations; at other times they are cultural, stemming from the values, ideologies, and biases that are prevalent in the cultural milieu in which the therapist was raised.

When we speak of characterological resistances we mean resistances having to do with being emotionally blocked in some way or another. Such resistances can result from narcissistic, hysterical, sadomasochistic, obsessive-compulsive, passive-feminine, phallic-narcissistic, or masculine-aggressive personality factors, for example, or from combinations of the above.

Narcissistic therapists may be resistant to confronting their

183

patients' grandiosity or rage and, as a result, may cultivate dependency and reinforce their patients' false selves. Hysterical therapists may want to avoid dealing with their patients' and their own erotic feelings, which means there is usually a lot of subtle sexual acting out that is not discussed and that may sabotage the relationship. Sadomasochistic therapists tend to shy away from expressions of tenderness–as do phallic-narcissists and masculine-aggressives–and may therefore keep their patients stuck at an angry place. Obsessive-compulsive therapists may not want to hear about certain traumatic events in their patients' lives that remind them of similar events on their own, while passive-feminine therapists tend to resist expressions of criticism or hostility towards themselves. Any characterological flaw with which a therapist has not at least become familiar can spell trouble in the therapy dyad.

Perhaps the worst of the characterological resistances are those stemming from character disorders in which symptoms are ego-syntonic and hence never recognized and worked through. For example, therapists might have a need to dominate and control their patients; in doing so they may be quite successful at unconsciously acting out primitive feelings of aggression, thereby maintaining a false sense of mastery and well-being that precludes their looking more deeply into themselves. Whenever a therapist's neurotic defenses *seem* successful, there will be a resistance to looking at them.

While characterological resistances by therapists are usually discussed in supervision, cultural resistances are often overlooked. It's important to recognize how much these resistances can also influence therapy negatively. It is generally more difficult for a supervisor to confront a supervisee about a bias than it is about a countertransference feeling that is being acted out.

One of the more prevalent and potentially harmful forms of cultural counterresistance comes about when therapists identify their selves–particularly their ideal selves–with a cause, a religion, or a mass movement. Those who identify with such a cause, movement, or religion—whether or not they are actually "card-carrying members"—will often become self-righteous (they are "right" and those outside the cause are "wrong"), in which case they will feel justified in transferring, resisting, and acting out aggressive feelings to such outsiders without feeling any guilt. In these cases, the cause, religion, or movement becomes a projection of the therapist's ideal image, while those parts of their selves they wish to disown are projected onto outsiders; they and their movement are "good" and outsiders are "bad." In the therapy dyad, when a therapist receives a patient who appears to be an outsider, the therapist may unconsciously resist certain material from this patient that the therapist considers "bad" or "wrong," thereby derailing the therapeutic process.

In recent times feminism has become such a cause. Those who identify their selves with feminism, women and men, often come to feel their way is the only way. They are "right," and those who do not accept the "gospel" of feminism are "wrong." Therapists who identify with feminism will resist male patients who they determine are "sexists," female patients who are "dupes," and any ideas contrary to feminist doctrine. In fact, feminist therapists sometimes perceive any threat to their belief system as an attack on their selves—which have become identified with the movement—and they will react with a narcissistic rage to all such threats. Because feminism is in vogue now and has become such an influential force, we have included several case histories demonstrating how it can lead to therapeutic resistances and impede progress.

Biases of various types also escape detection in supervision. They are, nevertheless, powerful sources of resistance by therapists. Biases can be racial, religious, sexual, ideological, national, or regional in nature. White therapists may have unconscious or not so unconscious biases towards blacks, which crop up as resistances in therapy, and likewise black therapists may have similar biases towards white patients. Male therapists may have biases towards females, and females towards males. Americans may have biases towards Bulgarians, and Bulgarians towards Americans. Liberals may have biases towards conservatives, and conservatives towards liberals. Northerners may have biases towards southerners and southerners against northerners. Jews may have biases towards Catholics, and Catholics towards Jews.

An urban northern therapist may have a patient who is a southerner from a rural environment who has a thick southern accent. The therapist, because of his cultural heritage, may have a bias with respect to southern accents and may find them offensive, which may bring about a general failure in his or her capacity to listen to and empathize with what the patient is saying. In addition, the therapist may also be unsympathetic to hearing about life in a rural, southern environment, due to built-in resistances having to do with stories about lynchings and the like that were current in his cultural milieu and frowned upon. The patient in such a setting will feel judged, will in some way withdraw, the therapy relationship will go nowhere.

We have selected a variety of case histories that reflect the range of counterresistance situations occurring regularly. When possible, we have shown how supervision or therapy has been helpful in rectifying these situations. Naturally, there will be many situations left out; this is not because we thought them unimportant but because within the scope of this book we needed to select those we were most familiar with. Perhaps our own resistances will come to the surface with respect to which were selected.

Finally, it is interesting to note that many of the therapists portrayed in these case histories were trained in the most prestigious institutes. Despite a rigorous weeding-out process of supposedly unhealthy candidates and an equally rigorous training analysis and case control supervision, counterresistances still prevail. The problem here is that what the members of an institute consider as a healthy personality can depend upon their particular biases; for example, traditional institutes will look for candidates who are more or less emotionally passive and who express opinions that coincide with the belief system current at the institute. Thus a candidate may appear to have "neutralized" his aggressive and erotic feelings and seem to have the "right" psychoanalytic viewpoint, when in fact that candidate may have severe, successfully repressed or sublimated, psychopathological aspects in their personality. There is the danger that institutes or schools of therapy can become—like the movements discussed before—dogmatic, self-righteous, and elitist in their attitude, assuming those from their school are "right" and all others are "wrong." Some of the histories that follow will, we hope, amplify this view.

CHAPTER FIVE

CHARACTEROLOGICAL COUNTERRESISTANCES

Blunder 62

The Female Therapist
and the Male Chauvinist Pig

A 25-year-old man had been in therapy with an older female therapist for several months when he began to focus on his difficulties with women.

"Basically," he said, "I hate American women. They're so bitchy and demanding and, if you ask me, spoiled. And it disgusts me the way they use feminism as an excuse to manipulate and control their husbands and boyfriends. I've decided, in fact, to only go out with foreign women. Oriental women, for instance. Now they really know how to treat a man. Yeah, that's what I need, a woman who won't be demanding and bitchy and who'll be there whenever I need her sexually. I've had it with American women."

His therapist, a mature woman who was not a political feminist, nevertheless was rather taken aback by such diatribes and could not respond to them with empathy. She found herself thinking that he was a "male chauvinist pig" and would make comments such as, "I see, you want somebody who'll be completely submissive to you," or "Yes, Oriental women aren't liberated the way American women are, so they're easier to dominate."

The therapist was narcissistically wounded by his attacks on

American women and was compelled to defend them and herself. That is, her self had become identified with women in general; hence an attack on American women was taken by her as an attack on herself. Yet, the more she made defensive statements to the patient, the more he lashed out on the subject. They became blocked, and the therapy took on the characteristics of a sustained argument.

Fortunately, she discussed the matter with her male supervisor, realizing that she felt personally attacked by the patient. With the supervisor's help, she was able to understand and then drop her resistance to his views about women and to empathize with the little boy who needed a patient, supportive, understanding mother surrogate.

The patient had had a very aggressive and seductive mother who would crawl into his bed at night, even into his middle teens, and sleep with him after a quarrel with his father. There was no physical contact of a sexual nature, but there was a great deal of emotional seduction. Hence the patient was frightened of demanding women, frightened not only of violating the incest taboo, but also of merging with his mother, being overwhelmed by her, and losing his gender identity—not to mention the arousal of his castration fear. Because of his insecurity around his gender identity, he was phallic-narcissistic in character and had to have intercourse more than once a day, often supplemented by masturbation. His masculinity was so threatened by relationships with even the most submissive women that he was filled with anxiety; even the most benign assertiveness frightened him.

When the patient began making sexual advances to the therapist, things reached a crucial point. Again the therapist was taken aback and felt anger welling inside her.

"What would it mean to you if I had sex with you?" she would ask him, trying to stick with a neutral, analytic stance.

"I don't know. Why don't we try it and see?"

He wasn't ready for analysis. He also sensed the therapist's disapproval of him, and it made him persist all the more with acting out his feelings and resisting the analysis. He was nowhere near the point where he could drop his defenses and examine his anxiety about his masculinity. Finally, after more discussions with her supervisor, the therapist began to back off. When the patient spoke of marrying an Oriental woman who could fulfill his needs, the therapist was able to be supportive, realizing that given this patient's psychopathology and his particular upbringing, such a marriage represented the most viable solution at the time.

Blunder 63

The Therapist Who Went to Sleep

A certain male patient had a way of talking, as he lay on the couch, that was like a drone. The sentences were all of the run-on variety, and there was never a place for the therapist, who was an older man, to get a word in. Invariably, the therapist felt bored during this patient's visits, and on a couple of occasions he even fell asleep.

On the second occasion in which he fell asleep, the patient happened to turn around, sensing something, and caught the therapist nodding in his chair.

"Are you asleep?" he asked, deeply offended.

"No," the therapist lied. "I just had my eyes closed."

"Oh. You looked like you were asleep."

"If you imagined I was asleep, what did you think about it? How did it make you feel?"

The therapist proceeded to go through this standard analytic procedure without ever acknowledging that he had, in fact, been asleep. Why? On the surface, it was because he didn't want to hurt the patient's feelings; on a deeper level it was because of his fear of his own and the patient's deeper feelings of rage and longing. The patient had a resistance to allowing the therapist to have any input into his innermost thoughts. It was as though the therapist did not even exist for him. What this stirred up in the therapist was a rage reaction; he felt rejected by the patient, shut out the way his own father had shut him out as a small child. Thus the patient's resistance produced in the therapist a counterresistance. The patient resisted contact with the therapist, and the therapist then resisted contact with the patient by falling asleep. If the therapist had attempted to analyze the patient's resistance to contact, he might have gradually opened the patient up. Instead he acted out his rage by falling asleep, and then compounded this injury by refusing to acknowledge to the patient what he had done.

A few months later the patient used the excuse of financial difficulty to leave therapy, and the therapist, still acting out a father counterresistance, gave the patient his blessings.

Blunder 64

The Grandiose Therapist
and the Grandiose Patient

Seven years. Seven years a particular male patient, now in his early forties, had been in therapy with a certain male therapist, now in his late fifties. And for all those years not very much had changed in the patient's life; the patient was still complaining about the same things. He was a moderately successful advertising copywriter who complained that he was a creative genius who should be writing the "great American novel." He was married to a warm, supportive woman, but he complained that he deserved somebody more attractive and more attentive. He never started a novel during the seven years of therapy nor had an affair with another woman in the fifteen years of his marriage.

The therapist reluctantly acknowledged that the patient wasn't making progress. He was forced to admit this to himself as he began to feel more and more irritable before, during, and after his sessions with the patient. What was the problem? In discussions with his supervisor he had to come to grips with his own and his patient's grandiosity.

The therapist in all these years had not pointed out the patient's obvious grandiosity because he was blind to his own. This was a patient who was in reality afraid to venture into creative writing or creative lovemaking because it would puncture the balloon of his conceit; he might find out that he wasn't who he pretended to be. And he was insufferable to both his wife and his co-workers because of this obvious characterological problem. The therapist had similar problems with respect to conceit; he had had considerable musical training and always felt he could have been a great concert pianist if he had felt like it, but he had decided to put his talents to use in a helping profession instead. As a therapist he also had many illusions about himself. He frequently spoke before large audiences at seminars and thought very highly of himself. However, colleagues did not necessarily share his own view of himself, and he was not that well liked. Consequently he had not reached the status he expected of himself, which he attributed to bad luck.

Because of his grandiosity, it was difficult for him to seek out and listen to a supervisor. He did so only because of his irritability at not only this patient but others as well. With the supervisor's help he gradually became aware of the counterresistance and was able to begin moving in the right direction in his work with the patient.

Blunder 65

The Therapist and the TV Star

A relatively young female therapist was fortunate enough to be referred a prominent television star as a patient. She felt so honored to have this patient that she handled the star differently than she did her other patients. She tried hard to please her, rarely confronted her, was extremely flexible about changing appointments, stayed late in order to see her, and was ingratiating. Often she would compliment the star on a recent role, acting more as a fan than a therapist.

As the result of this behavior by the therapist, the patient formed a collusion with her; the therapist told the patient how wonderful a star she was, and the star told the therapist what a wonderful therapist she was, and neither of them ever mentioned any negative feelings they might have about one another. Hence the star's transference and resistance never got analyzed (because of the counterresistance of the therapist to do so).

The therapist was a good example of a person who is self-effacing as a defense against grandiosity. It was difficult for her to take in compliments or speak positively about herself, due to chronic low self-esteem rooted in an infantile relationship with her mother in which she felt disapproved of. She needed to be attached to this star in order to enhance her self-esteem through narcissistic extension. The star represented her mother – the omniscient, glamorous mother of early childhood – and instead of being idealized by the patient, she herself did the idealizing. In doing so, she fed the star's narcissistic need for idealizing and attention.

And so they went on for many months with the same ritual.

"You were the best one in the movie," the therapist would tell her. "Very in touch with your feelings."

"I'm so lucky to have you as a therapist," the star would say.

"Oh, I don't know about that. Anybody could work with you."

Continually working through her counterresistance in her own therapy and supervision was eventually helpful in resolving the therapist's errors.

Blunder 66

The Therapist Who Did Not Want To Be Superior

In at least one sense therapists must be superior to their patients: in order to help their patients, therapists must have advanced therapeutically or maturationally beyond the levels of their patients. Otherwise they would not possess the objectivity necessary to be truly helpful. In addition, many patients have a *need* to idealize their therapists, to see them as superior, especially during the early part of the treatment.

There was a therapist, however, who did not want to feel superior to his patients and who was therefore resistant to being idealized by them. This resistance on his part stemmed from both cultural and characterological factors. He was raised in a culture that stressed egalitarianism; according to the value system in this culture, all human beings were equal, and one should never feel superior to anybody in any respect whatsoever, much less acknowledge it. This man took this philosophy so far that when, for example, he played tennis he would never engage in actual games for fear that one person would then have to win and another lose — one would be inferior and one superior. Characterologically, this attitude was rooted in a defense against feelings of grandiosity that first appeared during his infancy.

Now it happened that a patient came into therapy, a very narcissistic patient, who had a marked emotional blockage and aloofness and a habit of shutting off interpretations. He would not listen to them, or he would seem to listen to them but would immediately forget them, or he would reply that they were irrelevant. At the same time, he continually complained that he wasn't getting any better. "I don't feel anything's happening. I don't *feel* anything. Least of all anything about you. I guess I should be feeling good about you or something. I should admire you. But I don't. Actually, I don't think you've given me anything at all."

As this situation continued session after session, the therapist listened tolerantly and patiently without defending himself or attacking the patient. As he did so, he was momentarily aware of the thought that it was, in fact, quite admirable of him to be able to listen tolerantly and patiently despite the fact that the patient rejected or nullified everything he said. However, he flinched as he thought this and immediately banished the thought from his mind. Then the thought occurred to him that, deep down, the patient really did admire him and was defending himself against such positive feelings about the therapist through his negative posture. The therapist was on the verge of making the interpretation but then stopped himself. At that moment a counterresistance to interpreting arose.

On the one hand it stemmed from a feeling of guilt and inhibition about speaking of his own virtues (his own superiority), and on the other hand from his identification with the patient's resistance against accepting a relationship with an object experienced as superior and good, since this implied his own inferiority and guilt. In addition, the therapist was also aware that if he made the interpretation, it might resolve the patient's resistance to accepting the therapist as a superior object, and that the patient might then develop an idealizing transference towards him; to this possibility he also had a counterresistance.

Fortunately, this therapist had had enough analysis to transcend his own cultural and characterological heritage; having become aware of his own resistances, he proceeded to give the proper interpretations during the next session, and the therapeutic relationship went back on course.

Blunder 67

The Therapist Who Encouraged Depression

A female therapist was seeing a successful male professional who was prone to severe depressions. She was always extremely sympathetic and compassionate towards his depression, always asking about it, about his insomnia, about his related disappointments, and repeatedly saying things such as "I know you must be in a lot of pain" and "I can understand how you must feel" and "I want you to know I really care about you." The man responded by staying depressed.

The effect of her sympathetic response to him was that it rewarded and encouraged his depression. He was basically a masochistic character who had gotten a great many secondary gains from his depressions. The therapist failed to analyze any of this—in fact, had a characterological counterresistance to analyze it—and after a while he became even more depressed and even went to the verge of suicide.

The therapist had had a disadvantaged younger brother—one who had a physical ailment as well as depression—and she had felt a great deal of compassion for his illness but also unconsciously preferred him to be ill rather than to have him successfully compete with her. She now transferred all of this onto her patient; on the surface she seemed to be sympathetic and supportive, but unconsciously she was keeping him depressed and neutralizing his possible competition with her. Also, in her compassion toward him she also expiated guilt toward her brother as well as to the patient.

This situation was eventually resolved because the patient was in group therapy with the same therapist, and some of the other patients in the group perceived what was happening and brought it to the attention of the therapist. At first she wanted to deny it.

"I don't think I'm rewarding his depression," she replied to them. "I'm just doing my job, just being empathic. Maybe you're jealous because you feel Tom's getting preferrential treatment. Could that be it?"

But the group persisted and after several weeks the therapist was able to acknowledge her own counterresistance to alleviating his depression. The patient then dropped out of therapy—the relationship had gone on too long and had been too destructive to him to continue; however, he admired the therapist's honesty and even referred one of his best friends to her for therapy.

Blunder 68

The Stoic Therapist

"My wife is so cold and rejecting," a male patient complained. "She is so damn nutty about independence that I can't ever lean on her, not even for a second."

"Don't be such a crybaby," his male therapist replied. "You can take care of yourself if you want to. You make too many infantile demands on your wife. Why don't you act like a man?"

Such was the essence of the relationship between this patient and therapist. The patient was continually attempting to get sympathy from the therapist, and the therapist was continually pushing him away. Like the patient's wife, the therapist would not let him lean on him.

One day—following the death of the patient's mother—the patient became quite upset at the therapist.

"You know, my mother's just died and even now I don't feel the slightest bit of sympathy from you. You haven't even offered me the most routine condolence."

"Why should *I* feel sad for you. It was *your* mother who died, not *mine*," the therapist coolly replied.

Obviously the therapist had a counterresistance. He was not at all receptive to helping this patient work through his oral fixations, due to his own unresolved needs. The therapist's mother had died when he was two years old; in order to survive he had had to repress his oral needs, feelings, and memories and defend against them through the development of a stoic character structure. In order to reinforce this defense, he even married a cold woman who totally lacked any maternal qualities. His disparagement of his patient's needs was in the service of maintaining a repression of the oral needs and protecting against what had to have been a devastating blow – his mother's death – to his sense of self.

However, the patient had had enough of this therapist's coldness. A few weeks after his own mother's death he terminated therapy.

Blunder 69

The Therapist and the Ugly, Disgusting Patient

The patient was a young woman in her thirties who had been to several therapists already. She had been a sexually abused child and as a consequence had a negative image of herself because of her guilt feelings about her sexual experiences. As the result of her previous therapy her external life had improved to a degree, but she still perceived herself, down deep, as an "ugly, horrible, disgusting creature." Again and again she spoke disparagingly about herself to her present therapist, an older woman. Not only did she feel ugly and disgusting, but she continually compared herself with her two sisters (she was the middle child), whom she felt were both beautiful. Neither of the two sisters had been abused.

The therapist, who was basically well analyzed and sophisticated analytically, nevertheless had a resistance to hearing the patient disparage herself and continually tried to divert her away from such themes, attempting to stress the positive. For example, she had the patient bring in photos of herself and her sisters, and then said to her, "You see, you are every bit as attractive as your sisters. In fact, you were a very, very cute little girl."

To the therapist's consternation, at the next session the patient was even more self-disparaging and said, "I've been thinking of leaving therapy. I don't think it's doing any good." The therapist encouraged her to elaborate on her feelings. "I don't know," she said. "I just don't feel very hopeful about my life or my future. I just bought a cottage in the country, and now I don't even know if I want it. I'm sure the termites are going to eat away at it until they destroy it anyway. A termite inspector's supposed to come this weekend, but I'm sure he'll probably tell me there are no termites in it, despite the fact that he will *know* there are termites there. I just don't feel hopeful that anything's going to work out."

The therapist did not at first understand the meaning of this communication by the patient; however, her supervisor suggested that what the patient was saying, indirectly, was that the therapist did not seem to understand her, was telling her she was attractive when the patient herself knew she was ugly (had termites). The therapist was simply trying to cover her psychic hurts with bandaids, as most of her previous therapists had tried to do.

Once the therapist understood the communication, she could acknowledge her counterresistance to hearing the patient disparage herself. There was a part of herself that did not want to get into the disgusting, ugly feelings of her patient or herself. The therapist had begun her own analysis with a self-image not dissimilar to the patient's. Although she had worked through a great many issues involving her primitive rage, her disgust with her own body, and her negative view of her self, there was enough left unresolved so that she unconsciously and, to some degree consciously, did not want to be reminded of her own problems by dealing with the patient's.

Understanding her own counterresistance enabled the therapist to continue with the patient and to truly listen to her. In helping the patient to work through her feelings, the therapist also was compelled to do further work on her own. The therapy dyad is always a mutually therapeutic relationship when it is working well.

Blunder 70

The Holistic Health Therapist

A certain female therapist was known in her circles as one of the gentlest and most humane creatures around. Although she was in her early thirties, she retained the look of an adolescent – she wore her hair in pigtails and used little makeup on her freckled face. She practiced a form of therapy that she called "transpersonal" and utilized supportive therapy, vitamins, meditation, and Eastern philosophy. She was a woman who abhorred violence of any kind, and who truly felt that "love is the answer."

A male patient came to see her complaining of how angry he was and speaking about all those in his life whom he planned to get revenge on. "Someday, all of them are going to get their shit crammed right back down their own throats," he would tell her.

She smiled at him gently, and changed the subject. "Tell me about something you feel good about in your life."

"I don't feel good about anything."

"Surely there must be something."

"No, nothing. Do you want to hear what I'm going to do to my ex-girlfriend?"

In fact, the therapist did not want to hear. She had a resistance to hearing anything that smacked of anger or violence. Her own upbringing had been violent, her father constantly battering her mother, and her mother constantly belittling the father. As she had grown up, she had fantasized about saving her father from her mother and from his own violent tendencies. In her unconscious mind, she felt that she might have been able to love her father the way he deserved to be loved—unlike her mother, who was castrating toward him. Now she played out that drama with her patients, attempting to save them from their violence through her love. However, in doing so she was denying her own violence, her own unresolved rage at her mother and father. This unconscious rage got acted out by her not allowing her patients to express anger or rage or thoughts of violence in her presence. By frustrating their need to ventilate such feelings, she was actually making them even more angry and violent, all in the guise of doing good.

The man who had come to see her and had spoken about his plans for revenge, for example, became more and more insistent about talking about his revenge schemes. The more the therapist resisted hearing such schemes, the more vocal he was about presenting them to her. He experienced her as being a rejecting mother, and hence became more and more angry at her. Eventually, he felt violent.

"You know," he said to her one day. "I find myself wanting to slug you sometimes."

"Slug me?" she whispered softly, gently. "Have you been taking your medication?"

"No. That stuff doesn't work with me."

"Have you been staying on your vitamin diet?"

"No. I don't believe in that."

"I don't see how you expect me to help you if you won't try the things I ask you to try."

"I don't need any of that stuff. What I need is to kill a few people. That all. There are a few jerks who have stepped on my face a few too many times, and I just need to annihilate a few of them. Then I'll feel fine."

"You know, I'm beginning to think I'm not the right therapist for you," the therapist said, feeling very anxious and frightened.

The patient smiled. "I think you're right."

This therapist could only work with a certain kind of patient—one who, like herself, was into denying his or her own aggression and looking at the world through rose-colored glasses.

Blunder 71

The Intellectual Therapist

When this therapist was a child his mother used to say to him, as so many mothers do, "Stop that crying or I'll give you something to really cry about." In fact, no form of honest emotional expression was tolerated in his family, either by his mother, who was a writer, or his father, who was an editor. Rather, he was encouraged to be a stoic and to pursue intellectual goals. Later, as an adolescent, he developed what Erik H. Erikson and others have called "the intellectual defense" against the sexual awakening that is part and parcel of the teenage years.

Still later, when he decided to become a therapist, he "chose" to become a classical psychoanalyst. In his work with patients he emphasized the intellectual aspects of therapy: he himself remained rigidly neutral and passive towards the patient and attempted to focus solely on the patient's psychic conflicts, always keeping things at the level of some kind of scientific investigation. He read voraciously and had one of the largest psychoanalytic libraries around; indeed, he was noted for being a psychoanalytic scholar.

However, he had a counterresistance to emotion, and he would tell his patients, "Freud abandoned hypnosis and abreaction because he found that it was ineffective." He tended to attract patients who, like himself, were resistant to feelings—in which case there was an unconscious agreement to keep the therapy on an intellectual plane. (His own therapist and supervisor were also quite intellectual and avoidant of feelings.) And when this therapist did come across a patient who, despite the therapist's resistance, began to scream or cry or in other ways emote, the therapist would always stop them.

"You seem upset," he would say, or "I think we need to look at this more clearly, with a more objective eye," or, "Are you all right?" Then again, more often than not he would greet any display of emotion with a stoney silence, as though he were saying, "All right, go ahead and indulge yourself if you must. I'll wait till this ugly storm passes." In just such a manner had his own emotionality as a child been treated by his parents.

Therapy is both an emotional and an intellectual experience—as are all human relationships; and to have only one or the other is to not be fully human. Because of this therapist's resistance to emotionality, he failed his patients in many ways.

Blunder 72

The Passive-Aggressive Therapist and the Passive-Aggressive Patient

A therapist sent the husband of a patient he was treating to a female therapist. This man – a middle-aged college professor who wore a beard and smoked a pipe – was a classic passive-aggressive. He never displayed any outward hostility, but was frequently late, held back positive feelings, was often impotent and disinterested in sex, and never, never understood why his wife frequently got so angry at him.

However, as the female therapist listened to the husband tell his side of the story, she had a difficult time perceiving what, if anything, was wrong with the patient. "My wife is always demanding, demanding, demanding," he told her. "And she's always putting me down if I don't give in to her demands, so naturally I have to retreat further and further. What can I tell you, she's a demanding bitch!" The female therapist was inclined to agree with her patient, and her therapy with him was basically supportive; she did not see the need to do any analysis of his character resistance. "I think you're right. I think she is demanding." They spent many of their sessions analyzing the man's wife.

What was happening? The therapist took the situation to her supervisor; he informed her that she was acting out a counterresistance. The therapist, like the patient, was frequently late, held back her feelings, and was generally disinterested in sex. Her husband had often accused her of being a passive-aggressive, especially when she forgot to do things for him that she had promised to do. The therapist resented being labeled as a passive-aggressive, and what she did not want to acknowledge about herself she did not want to see in her patient. The supervisor's making her aware of the problem was, in this case, only of limited usefulness, because the therapist continued to deny her character defense, as in the case when such defenses are ego-syntonic.

Eventually she encouraged the patient to terminate therapy, concluding that it was almost entirely his wife's problems that caused conflict in their marriage.

Blunder 73

The Therapist Who Denied His Own Obesity

A woman who weighed over 250 pounds went to see a male therapist who was himself some forty pounds overweight. The woman had made a few attempts to deal with her obesity in a behavioral way, but had not really stuck to it. She had also made some abortive forays into psychoanalytic types of therapy without any major success. Now she was going to get into a deep psychoanalytic treatment "for real." However, she entered the new therapy relationship talking about how her obesity was not really her problem.

"My health's really quite good despite my weight, and I have as many men attracted to me sexually as I can handle," she told the therapist. "My problems have more to do with my irresponsibility about my free-lance work, my anger at my parents, and my inability to follow through with things. I think it's called procrastination."

The therapist agreed with her about her obesity. "I think people make too much of it."

The therapist was a man who would not be called obese; however, he was overweight, especially being that he was a short, small-boned man; yet his own self-image was that he was perhaps five pounds overweight instead of forty, and that it did not affect his health, his attractiveness, or his athletic ability. When he huffed and puffed on the tennis court and his opponent suggested that he might do better if he lost a few pounds, the therapist would say his weight had nothing to do with his shortness of breath. It was just a matter of conditioning.

In essence, the therapist was using the same defensive technique – denial – as his patient. His counterresistance kept him from noting the rather obvious fact that his patient was extremely obese and that it was causing problems for her both in terms of her health and her relationships. He was reluctant to confront her, analytically, about her denial because to do so would have meant confronting his own. So both of them did an "Emperor's New Clothes" number, and the patient got nowhere in her therapy. She finally left him, claiming he did not understand her.

Blunder 74

To Numb Out or Not To Numb Out

A patient was complaining about feeling "numbed out."

"What do you mean by 'numbed out'?" asked his therapist.

He replied, "I mean, I'm numbing myself so I don't feel my feelings. It seems to happen to me every time somebody's about to leave me. Like right now my girlfriend is about to go off on this trip. I don't know what I'm feeling. I guess I don't want to know."

The patient did not want to feel either the rage or the loneliness of abandonment, which went back to a time in his early childhood when his mother suddenly left him. He began to speak of other things, his mind was wandering, and an aura of detachment fell over him. The therapist saw all this happening, but did nothing. He let the patient wander for a long time while finding it more and more difficult to listen to him. At one point he became so bored with the patient that his own mind began wandering, and then he felt himself "numbing out." Suddenly he snapped to attention, realizing that his feelings (or lack thereof) were a clue to what was going on countertransference-wise.

I should be calling the patient's attention to his feelings, but I'm not, he thought. Why? He began a silent self-analysis and discovered that he was acting out a counterresistance. It happened that his own wife was also going off on a trip in the near future. He, like the patient, often defended himself against his feelings of anger and loss through "numbing out;" in fact, he was doing it right now. He did not want to deal with his own primitive feelings around abandonment; therefore he did not want to help the patient deal with *his*.

Once the therapist had gone through this minianalysis, he was able to regain his feelings and to help the patient to do likewise. Before long both had tears in their eyes.

Blunder 75

The False Therapist and the False Patient

The patient was a 35-year-old man who came from a very deprived background. His mother was a psychotic who was in and out of mental hospitals throughout his childhood; his father was an alcoholic who was never able to support the family. Neither was there for him; instead, he had to be there for each of them. Subsequently he had to develop what Alice Miller and others have called a "false self"—a self geared to the needs of his parents—while repressing his "real self," that is, his real feelings of anger, hurt, sadness, disappointment with regard to his relationship to his parents. This in turn resulted in his having, in essence, a false or sham relationship with his parents. His early life was full of poverty and shame about his parents, and he used to lie to his peers about his situation and about his feelings. However, by dint of hard work and superior intelligence, he became quite successful and relatively affluent as an adult, while maintaining the need to exaggerate his success and deny his inner feelings of shame and loneliness. Though he was generally pleasant and affable, it was really quite impossible for anyone to get very close to him. His need to keep protecting himself against humiliation caused him to keep people at a distance. He never had an intimate relationship with either a man or woman.

His therapist was a woman who in many ways had similar dynamics and defenses. She too had come from an impoverished background which included a psychotic parent who was a source of great humiliation. Her father was noted as the local buffoon, and he used to constantly make a spectacle of himself, while her mother was a weak, schizoid personality. The therapist also presented a "false self," a facade she had been forced to develop in order to relate to these parents, but which in her adult life kept people from really knowing her (for example, she always had a smile on her face, as though all were well with her). However, she had had a lot of analysis and had worked through much of the material associated with her defenses.

She found herself feeling very protective towards this particular patient. She was aware that he had a false self, that he often lied to her, and that he was sabotaging himself by keeping people at a distance and limiting himself to virtually an "observer" status in life. Yet she could not get herself to attack his facade and force him to be real with her, for she knew too well that he would then be confronted with an almost overwhelming amount of rage, sadness, and shame from his past humiliations. Also, she did not want once again to have to confront her own similar pain. Hence, the therapy relationship was largely a supportive one which, in fact, served to reinforce the man's defenses and to help him become even falser.

In talking to her supervisor about the case, she became aware of her counterresistance to dealing with his (and her own) pain. The supervisor suggested that it might be wise to put the patient in an active, confrontational therapy group, while she continued to see him individually. She did as her supervisor advised, placing him in a colleague's therapy group while continuing to see him twice a week on an individual basis. The group did attack his defenses almost immediately, and he might have left the group had it not been for the support he got from the therapist in his individual sessions. The combination was precisely what he needed. Before long he began to "come out" in the group and in his individual therapy and express his long-buried pain.

Blunder 76

The Therapist
Who Couldn't Stop Idealizing Her Brother

A certain male patient, who was a very dynamic and successful man in his forties, reminded his older female therapist of her brother, whom she had always idealized. This patient, while he was to some extent quite brilliant, was also quite authoritarian and conceited, thoroughly disliked by both his peers and his subordinates; his wife and children found him equally intolerant and intolerable. However, the therapist, in contrast, listened with rapt attention to his boasting, expressed admiration for him, and was apparently blind to his obvious grandiosity and sadism.

The therapist had had an abusive father and a weak mother; the only figure she could look up to in her childhood was her older brother, who was ten years older. Throughout her childhood he had acted as a mentor toward her and explained much about politics and economics to her. In retrospect she realized that in a sense she had been a captive audience for his narcissistic displays of his intellectual brilliance and that these displays were often accompanied by a rather disparaging attitude toward her and her own capabilities. Nevertheless, she overlooked these negative aspects of the relationship and denied her own feelings of anger toward him in order to continue to receive his positive attention and to be able to admire him and utilize him as a role model.

The fact that this patient reminded her of her brother certainly occurred to the therapist, but she was selectively inattentive to it. Whenever this patient came in for his sessions, she had the feeling that she was "sitting at the feet of the master," just as she had with her brother. Since she had the need to preserve her brother as an idealized male figure in her internal world, she did not really attack this patient's phallic narcissistic character structure, his grandiosity, or his sadism. Eventually the patient began to complain that nothing was happening in the therapy. He had originally come to therapy because of his interpersonal difficulties associated with feelings of rage that people were not appreciating his genius. While she herself had appreciated his genius, she had not helped him to find out why practically nobody else did.

The therapist became increasingly angry that the patient did not appreciate her admiration; this drove her back into supervision. She came to grips with her counterresistance to deidealizing the patient (and her brother) and having to confront his rage. Subsequently, she was able to begin being more confrontational with the patient.

Blunder 77

The Complainers

Often when a resistance–counterresistance relationship develops in therapy it is because of a confluence of characterological defenses. Such was the case when a young man with many personal assets, but whose main problem was that he was a chronic complainer, went into therapy with an older male therapist who was also a complainer.

The patient was a masochistic character, a "kvetch without a cause." His therapist had been encouraged repeatedly by his supervisor to attack this patient's character defenses (his chronic complaining); the therapist did this reluctantly and half-heartedly. He, too, was a masochistic character, although he had done a lot of working through in his own therapy. His mother and his father were both complainers, and he had seen very little but martyrdom as a role model. Despite much therapy his basic masochistic pattern persisted.

He complained to his supervisor that he had been attacking his patient's defenses and the patient was getting angry at him.

"Good," replied the supervisor. "The patient's character is a defense against his primitive rage. Naturally, when you attack his character, you'll get his rage."

"But I don't want his rage. I'm frightened of his rage. What if he leaves therapy? Maybe I should just go back to doing supportive therapy with him."

"If you do, you'll just be wasting your time and his. You'll be supporting his defense, rather than puncturing it and helping him to become real."

The therapist shook his head. "I don't know what to do. I guess I'll try."

"Why are you so afraid he'll leave?" the supervisor asked. This question led to the core of the matter: the therapist had never completely worked through his anger toward his mother. Instead of experiencing his anger at his mother's martyrdom, he had incorporated her character and now acted out the rage the same way she did—by bottling it up and complaining about his life. The therapist had always been afraid to get angry at his mother for fear she would leave him. Now he was afraid of attacking this patient's defenses for the same reason.

Without considerable supervision, this therapist might have gone on for years supporting the patient's defenses. This kind of situation is, unfortunately, quite common. Many patients are content to spend their sessions complaining, getting a certain comfort out of having a sympathetic response. Sometimes, with narcissistic patients, this is even a necessary condition of therapy for a while. But eventually the character defenses must be attacked if the patient is truly to grow.

Blunder 78

The Therapist Who Forgot an Appointment

She had come into therapy because of acute anxiety attacks having to do with separation from her mother and an older sister. She was the youngest in her family and had always felt invisible. Her older sister was a "star" who received all the attention for her ice skating skills and her musical talent, while the patient was treated as an afterthought, never given recognition in her own right. It was an attempt to do something creative in her own right—joining a writing workshop at the age of 26—which precipitated her anxiety attacks.

Her therapy went well because her therapist, a woman about ten years older than she, was able to identify strongly with her and give her the support she needed to break from her mother and older sister. After two years she was accepted into a prestigious graduate school program in creative writing and was engaged to be married. The therapist and the patient decided she was ready to terminate.

However, the therapist was resistant to explore with the patient her feelings about separation. The patient's last appointment was scheduled for 2 P.M. on a Friday afternoon, the day before her wedding. The therapist forgot the appointment and scheduled another patient for the same hour. At 1:50 the buzzer rang, the patient entered, and the therapist realized her mistake. When the second patient arrived, she rescheduled her appointment.

"I'm very, very sorry about this," the therapist said as she sat down in her chair to face the patient who was leaving. "You must feel very disappointed about this."

The patient could not speak. Tears were streaming down her cheeks, and she would not look at the therapist.

"Really I'm sorry. This is my fault; I've been denying to myself that you're leaving therapy. This whole thing happened because of my own trouble separating. That's why I identified with you so much and have become so attached to you; we share so many things, so many, many things. You see, I've never really resolved my own fears about abandonment and feelings around separations. And I suppose I've also been feeling angry at you for leaving me, and my forgetting your appointment was also an acting out of that anger. Anyway, I guess I just wanted to deny it all, pretend it wasn't happening. I'm so sorry you were hurt by this. And the really sad thing about it is that this whole episode is probably a replay of what has happened to you all your life, when nobody ever noticed you, when you were always the forgotten child."

The patient was tearful and quiet for a moment. "Thank you for your acknowledging your mistake," she said smiling. "And thank you for understanding me. I don't think I've ever felt so understood in my life."

The two women stood and hugged, both breaking into sobs, and parted warmly.

Usually it is not recommended that a therapist be this revealing; however, there are exceptions to every rule. During the termination phase of therapy revelations are much more appropriate—in fact *de rigeur*—and it is often at the termination phase that otherwise proficient therapists fail, because they are unable to come out of their neutral stance, unable to be real. The fact that the therapist in this case was able to catch herself and be real allowed for the proper closure. When the termination goes well, it usually involves the therapist's coming out of the neutral stance and becoming a fellow human being to some extent or another, and the parting is more like that of two friends than that of a therapist and a patient.

Blunder 79

The Therapist Who Could Not Stop Interpreting

A young male patient never responded positively to the interpretations of his female therapist. Sometimes he would reply outright, in a tone of annoyance, "That's off the wall. You're not helping me." Or he would simply continue free-associating without responding to her comments. This patient was highly narcissistic, and what he needed from his therapist—particularly during the early stages of therapy—was simply a holding environment, a place where he could express things that he had never been able to express before—especially with his own mother, who was judgmental. Each time the therapist made an interpretation, no matter how mildly she worded it, he experienced the interpretation as a judgment, that is, as his mother attacking him and saying he was bad.

However, the therapist also had narcissistic features in her character, and each time the patient rejected an interpretation she felt wounded, as though the patient were saying to her that her interpretations were worthless (her milk was worthless). An unconscious anger built up towards the patient, and she began giving more and more interpretations. In her own childhood, she had been the youngest of five children, and nobody ever wanted to hear her opinions about anything; in fact, one of her primary (unconscious) reasons for becoming a therapist was to gratify the need to prove that her opinions and her self were indeed valuable. Now she had run into another object (older sister representative) who put down her opinions.

Eventually the patient's resistance to hearing interpretations and the therapist's counterresistance to heeding the patient's complaints led to heated arguments between the two. The patient felt cornered: either he had to hear interpretations that made him feel bad, or he would have to quit therapy (which would also make him feel bad). In fact, it was the therapist's unconscious intention to do just that. In her narcissistic rage, she wanted to destroy this sibling rival by putting him in a no-win situation. She no longer wanted to relate; she wanted to conquer.

When the patient angrily terminated therapy she at first felt relieved. Only later, after she had analyzed the situation, did she feel remorse about the loss of the patient.

Blunder 80

The Therapist
Who Did Not Want To Upset His Mother

A novice therapist had had a very hysterical, manipulative mother. If he did not do and think and feel exactly how she wanted him to, she would have a hysterical temper tantrum, replete with anxiety attacks, heart palpitations, and headaches; the therapist's father would then tell the boy, "See what you've done to your mother?"

Now it happened that a female patient very much like the therapist's mother came into treatment with him. She was actually older than the therapist and took a maternal attitude towards him, giving him advice on matters of nutrition and hygiene. On some level he knew that the patient was manipulating him by condescending to him in this way, yet he did not confront her about it for fear of upsetting her. Nor did he confront her about the fact that she continually manipulated everybody else in her life, particularly her husband and children. Like the therapist's mother, this woman would have temper tantrums if the husband or children did not do as she wanted. For example, one evening the patient wanted her husband to take her dancing. He complained that he was tired from a day of work, his arthritic knees were acting up, and he did not like the orchestra. She became hysterical, accusing him of never thinking of anybody but himself, and of being a passive "wimp" who never wanted to leave his home because he was so afraid of people. She threw clothing and ashtrays, pounded her fists against the arms of the chair she was sitting on, and sobbed and sobbed until her children came to her aid and told the father, "Oh, why don't you take her dancing, Dad? It won't kill you. Just this once, for the sake of harmony in the household."

The therapist heard such things and would feel quite anxious and sometimes furious, but he said nothing. He smiled and nodded and the patient would smile and nod, and it was as though the two were in perfect agreement. The therapist was not only afraid of upsetting her (his mother) but also of losing her approval. They had formed a collusion—a resistance–counterresistance collusion; she treated him as though he were the good son she wished she had, one who always understood her and supported her no matter what, and he in turn treated her as she wished to be treated—he gave her unconditional acceptance. Thus each fulfilled his or her neurotic needs in the relationship. He got the approval from her that he never got from his mother, and she got the unconditional acceptance from him that she never got from her father.

Meanwhile the symptoms that had driven her to therapy remained the same: she continued to drink heavily, continued to feel angry and dissatisfied about her intimate relationships, and continued to feel unfulfilled as a human being.

Blunder 81

The Therapist
Who Resented Being a Truant Officer

Borderline patients can often demand a lot of a therapist's attention during the beginning phase of treatment, which may last for several years.

One such patient became quite vexing to her therapist. She was a young woman who had problems in just about all aspects of her life; she was fired from job after job, she was always on some drug or another (cocaine, marijuana, alcohol, or mescaline), and her relationships with the people around her, including family and lovers, tended to be extremely sadomasochistic. She began each session complaining that she didn't want to be in therapy, that it wasn't going to help her, and she was hopeless. She generally came late to sessions, and every now and then, when she went on a binge, she would skip a few sessions altogether. In addition, she often forgot to bring her money for sessions.

Her therapist tried to maintain therapeutic neutrality but found himself growing more and more irritated at her.

"What do you think it's about, that you keep coming late and that you sometimes skip sessions," he would say to her, attempting to analyze the resistance.

"I don't know." She would squirm around on the couch. "Do you think I should see my boyfriend again? I really think I ought to break off with him."

"You changed the subject."

"Did I? What were we talking about?"

"I asked you what it was about that you come late and skip appointments frequently."

She tossed this way and that on the couch, sighing. "Oh, God, I guess because I don't want to be here. I don't know, maybe the thing for me to do is just go commit suicide."

The therapist was in a hurry to analyze the patient, despite the fact that the patient was nowhere ready for analysis. He was in a hurry for several reasons. He had just recently graduated from an analytic institute and wanted to apply what he had learned, wanted to get to the heart of the matter, to the infantile material, to the transference, to the resistances. He felt that, instead of being a psychoanalyst, he was a truant officer. "If I'd wanted to be a truant officer, I would have trained to be one," he told himself. He resented having to set boundaries for patients such as this one, although that is precisely what she needed. In order to treat such patients, a therapist literally has to go down into the "trenches" with them and "slug it out" at their level until they come to grips with how they are behaving. Often, therapists need to express how angry and how hopeless such patients are making them feel, and when the therapist does so, it helps to show the patient what impact she is having on them. It also frees the patient up to express such feelings directly herself.

However, the setting up of boundaries must be done from the beginning in order for it to work. Once patients have been allowed to act out for a considerable period of time, they are reluctant to give up what they see as their "rights." In the present case, the therapist indeed waited too long to "put his foot down." His resistance to being a truant officer, which to him meant being a tyrant, was so great that he waited until he was too immobilized by rage to act effectively. When he attempted to do so, it was in an angry, judging way, a way that conveyed to the patient that he felt she was persecuting him.

"I'm sorry," he told her. "I just can't tolerate this kind of behavior anymore."

Unfortunately, his tone and manner were too similar to her father's and *his* father's at that point, and she did not return to therapy again after that.

CHAPTER SIX

CULTURAL COUNTERRESISTANCES

Blunder 82

The White Trash Therapist and the Debutante

He was a therapist who had to work himself up the hard way. He was born in a ghetto in Detroit, in one of the few white families in a predominantly black neighborhood. He had suffered in many ways; his parents were both alcoholics, scarcely able to support their seven children, of which he was the fourth; he felt lost in the shuffle as far as getting any parental attention; and at school, being one of only three white students in a black school, he felt continually persecuted and invalidated and picked up the nickname, "White Trash." Through a lot of determination he managed to work his way through a community college and then get into a Ph.D. program in psychology, again working his way through by doing factory work in Detroit auto firms. He moved to New York to attend a psychoanalytic institute and set up practice.

One of his first patients was a debutante. She was an attractive young woman who had made her debut into Boston society when she was seventeen. Her ancestry could be traced to the Mayflower. She drove a Porsche, had her own airplane, and owned an estate in Connecticut. She lived the life of the jet set. Obviously, she had many things going for her; however, she had a great deal of anger at men, partly because of having been sexually abused by an uncle, and partly because of her mother's favoritism of her two brothers. This anger at men wreaked havoc on her relationships, which tended to be one-night stands. She also tended to drink too much and was bulimic.

In her therapy she tended to be rejecting of the therapist, being condescending and castrating, just as she tended to be with the men in her life. A repeated theme was her telling the therapist she did not think he could understand her, primarily because they came from different walks of life. She came from a "society background," but about him she would say, "You're not from society; let's put it that way." Because the therapist had deep feelings about coming from an impoverished "white trash" family, he developed a counterresistance. On some level he understood that she was testing him to see if she could trust him, but he refused to give her that understanding. Instead, he defended himself and subtly counterattacked her.

"No, I'm not from high society, but I don't think you have to be from high society to understand somebody's psychological conflicts."

"Well, you would think that, since you're not from society."

"Aren't you being a tad snobby?"

"No, I don't think so."

"All right. Fine. Then I don't understand you. Have it your way."

"Are you sulking? You men are such little boys sometimes."

"You perceive me as sulking? Is that what you'd like – to make me sulk, to take away my manhood and make me a sulking little boy?"

"Oh, you're always analyzing. Always, always. What am I going to do with you? Must you be so defensive?"

Once having been put on the defensive in this way he had lost control of the therapeutic relationship; he was not able to confront her about her need to reject, snub, condescend to, castrate, and exclude all the men in her life, to act out the anger stemming from her childhood fixations. Nor was he able to empathize with the abused little girl who was seeking a man she could trust. He had a resistance to understanding her on a human level, just as she had a resistance to understanding him on that level. They had each become malevolent transference objects for one another and were locked in combat to prove each other wrong.

Had the therapist been more resolved about his impoverished background, he might have been more on top of his counterresistance feelings, in which case he could have given the patient the empathy and the gentle confrontation she needed in order to come to grips with her compulsion to repeat. Unfortunately, he was not able to do so, and the therapy ended after a few months.

Blunder 83

The White Liberal
Therapist and the Black Patient

Although a young black male patient continually brought in dreams that indicated a great deal of mistrust and suspiciousness concerning his white male therapist, the therapist was resistant to interpreting these dreams in terms of the racial issue. Instead, the therapist repeatedly interpreted these dreams as transference reactions to him and derivative of early feelings to his parents.

There were often pauses in their dialogue. At these times the patient was frequently wondering if this white man could truly understand him; yet, out of politeness he said nothing about it. The therapist was usually quick to interpret these pauses as due to a resistance to getting in touch with unconscious material. The relationship went on this way for a year, and the therapist helped the patient work on problems in his career situation. At the end of the year they terminated amicably.

"Thank you. You've really helped me a lot," the black man said, shaking the therapist's hand warmly, smiling.

"I'm glad I've been of help. You did most of it yourself," the therapist responded in an equally warm manner.

In truth, neither felt very warmly towards the other and nothing real had happened in their relationship. The patient had been resistant to bring up the racial issue, wanting to impress the therapist with how progressive and "unblack" he was. The therapist had a counterresistance to bringing up the matter because he had a need—which for the most part was unconscious—to think of himself as a liberal and a humanitarian and hence oblivious to what color a man's skin was. The therapist had, in fact, come from a long line of Boston liberals, all of whom had put much stock in championing causes such as equal rights for minorities. In this circle it was considered a *faux pas* to acknowledge any differences between blacks and whites; a black was simply another human being, and to bring up his blackness or suggest that his culture was different would be an admission of prejudice.

And so, in the name of human rights, this therapy relationship ended the way it had begun: a sham.

Blunder 84

The Feminist Therapist

A young woman went to a female therapist, who advertised herself in the local newspaper as a "feminist therapist," and complained to the therapist that her husband continually battered her.

"You've come to the right person," the therapist said empathically. "I've helped lots of women like yourself. Don't worry, I'll tell you exactly what to do."

The therapist proceeded to help the patient move out, first placing her in a women's shelter, then helping her find her own apartment. She also assisted her in pressing charges against her husband for assault and battery and taking other legal actions. After about six months the therapist suggested that the patient was doing all right and did not need therapy anymore, and the patient agreed. The patient thanked the therapist profusely for the help, they hugged, and she left feeling quite grateful and strong. A few months later she met another man, quite similar to the one she had just separated from, and moved in with him. Before long he had begun to batter her just as the previous man had done. Obviously, the therapist had not helped the patient to resolve the underlying psychic conflicts that led to her difficulties.

The patient was a very angry and provocative woman who was unconsciously castrating towards the men with whom she became involved. Her provocative and castrating behavior invariably induced a rage reaction from the men (who were prone to violence anyway). She was drawn to violent men like her father, while her mother, who had also been a battered woman, had modeled the role of the helpless martyr. Therefore, throughout her childhood she had been trained to have masochistic relationships with men and knew no other kind. The feminist therapist had not helped her at all to resolve this masochism.

The therapist had a resistance to seeing the patient's characterological problems. As a feminist, she harbored the view that men were oppressors and women were victims. Even when a woman, say, murdered a man, this therapist would find reasons why the woman was driven to it by oppression; while if a man committed any act of violence or the like it was always because he was simply "bad," simply a villain. There was no capacity on her part to understand that the man, too, might have been driven to it. The therapist had never resolved her narcissistic rage connected to the events of her childhood, a rage that now had become transferred onto men in general; and the cultural atmosphere of the times, in which feminism was predominant, reinforced this rage at men. The therapist acted out her rage by using situations such as the one provided by this patient as a vehicle to go on a "witch hunt" for "male chauvinist pigs." She had a need to see herself and her patient as "right" and "innocent," hence a resistance to considering the patient's contribution to her dilemma or looking at her masochistic character structure.

And so the patient continued her compulsive pattern, continued the vicious cycle, a cycle that had gone on for generations in her family and would now most likely be passed on to her own children.

Blunder 85

The Draft Dodger and the Viet Nam Veteran

During the Viet Nam War this therapist had been a college student who had protested militantly against the war, burned his draft card in public, sat in jail for several days and, eventually, had lived in Canada for a few years to escape the draft.

A man came to see him complaining of drug problems, violent behavior with his girlfriend, and problems holding on to jobs. The therapist listened empathically and patiently to the details of all these complaints for several sessions. Then, on the fourth session, the patient revealed that he was a Viet Nam veteran. He looked up at the therapist, expecting a sympathetic response.

"Oh, yes?" the therapist said.

"I've never been the same since the war."

"I see."

"I have nightmares about it all the time."

"I see."

"Is something the matter?"

"No. Why?"

"You look funny."

The therapist did, indeed, look funny. His face had turned

pale and his brows had furrowed and his arms had folded. The therapist was beset by a mixture of feelings – guilt about having dodged the war, contempt for this man for having been foolish enough to go there, and anger at the patient for putting him on the spot and "begging" for his sympathy. He also felt contemptuous because the patient came from a different cultural milieu – a conservative, blue collar stratum – and spoke with a heavy city accent. Finally, he could sense the man's intense rage and was fearful that the patient would sense the therapist's contempt for him and would transfer that rage onto the therapist and become violent. All of this combined to give the therapist a resistance to this patient that was so strong he could not go on.

"Is everything all right?" the patient asked.

"Actually, no. I'm afraid I'm going to have to recommend that you see another therapist. This just isn't going to work out. I can feel too much antagonism between us from the beginning. I'm sorry. There's no charge for this session. Good luck."

With that he shook the patient's hand. The patient left with a puzzled expression on his face.

The therapist had done the right thing. He knew that his countertransference and counterresistance were too strong and his fear too intense for him to work successfully with the patient. However, the confrontation with this patient brought to his attention an issue he still needed to resolve in his own therapy; until it was successfully resolved, he would have to limit his practice to certain types who were compatible with him. To be sure, practically all therapists do this. However, sometimes due to glaring characterological defenses or cultural biases such limitations are more severe than necessary.

Blunder 86

The Therapist Who Feared Dependency

A young woman patient was constantly manipulated by her older male therapist, who was devoted to what he called "progressive analysis," a form of analysis he had learned at a "progressive institute" that featured a short-term approach to treatment. Specifically, this therapist was determined to keep her from developing a regressive dependency on him, and he would be openly critical about the hazards of classical analysis, which he warned often kept people in a state of infantile dependency for years. (He had, of course, never worked through his own infantile transference feelings, and so was resistant to such feelings from his patient.)

Hence, for this particular patient his technique was aimed at not allowing any long silences to occur, giving a great deal of encouragement, and keeping the atmosphere of the treatment hour lively, cheerful, and nonconfrontational. When the patient became sexually involved with a much older man, the therapist insisted she was showing improvement and encouraged the relationship. He did not see his manipulations as an expression of his own instinctual needs, as well as a hostility towards psychoanalysis, nor did he recognize that the patient's affair was not true independence but a form of submission to him as well as an acting out of her sexual transference, which he failed to analyze.

A few months into this affair the patient decided she was ready to leave treatment, and the therapist encouraged the termination, seeing it as a sign of maturity and independence.

"I think you've more or less achieved what you set out to achieve," he assured her.

And so the patient left treatment and proceeded to have a succession of affairs with older men, acting out without resolving her transference feelings, while the therapist congratulated himself on another "short-term therapy" success. This is but one example of how a school of therapy can become a counterresistance.

Blunder 87

The "Straight"
Therapist and the Homosexual Patient

"I had this weird, embarrassing dream about you last night," an attractive young female patient said to her therapist, who was also an attractive female. "I don't know what it means. It was kind of sexual." The therapist, usually quite responsive, particularly to any mention of a dream, was silent. "I've never understood why I've always developed these intense crushes on women," the patient continued. "I've done it all my life. Maybe I'm a lesbian. What do you think? Do you think I'm a lesbian?"

"Don't worry. It doesn't mean that. You're not a lesbian," the therapist quickly replied. The therapist was in a haste to end the subject, for it aroused a great deal of anxiety in her; in doing so she effectively and unwittingly closed the door on the topic and blocked her patient's progress for several months.

The therapist came from an extremely poor, Jewish family that had a tradition of scholastic achievement among its men. While in her twenties, with two children to support, the therapist decided to make a career in social work and entered therapy as part of her training. Her issues had to do with belonging: being Jewish, she felt she did not fully belong in a predominantly Christian society; nor did she feel she belonged in her own family, with its subordination of females to males. Her developing a successful career as a therapist and her identification with the women's movement gave her a sense of belonging.

Now she was treating this patient, who was also in training to be a therapist and who wanted to make an issue out of whether or not she was a lesbian. The therapist was resistant to hearing about this issue for several reasons. On a conscious level she was afraid the younger woman would lose everything—i.e., that she would not belong anymore if she came out as a lesbian. On a deeper level the patient's doubts about her sexuality aroused similar doubts that the therapist had with respect to her own sexuality and femininity, doubts that were never analyzed in her own therapy, for her therapist had a similar resistance to dealing with homosexual material.

Only once again, a few months later, did the patient bring the subject up, and once again the therapist replied, hastily, "You're not a lesbian, okay? Stop worrying already."

She was unable to help this patient, whose homosexual fantasies had to do with important preoedipal material crucial to her personal life and her professional development. This whole area would remain an uncharted sea for the younger therapist (as it had for the older one), who would then continue the cycle with her own patients.

Blunder 88

The German Therapist
and the Holocaust Victim

A therapist of German origin, who had come to America as a boy before Hitler had come to power, nevertheless felt a great deal of guilt about the German atrocity. This "cultural" guilt was never worked through in his training analysis.

Later, when he had set up practice in Boston, one of the patients who came to see him was a middle-aged woman who had been a small child during the Nazi era and had been put in a concentration camp. There she had been sexually abused, was forced to help dig a grave that eventually her mother was buried in, and had almost died of starvation. Fortunately, the Allies released all prisoners just before she reached death. She survived, but not without deep psychic wounds.

Ostensibly, she came to the therapist because of a depression she felt was related to the recent death of her husband of thirty years. The therapist was wonderfully empathic about the husband's death, and quite helpful with respect to that mourning process. However, her depression did not go away, and eventually she began to talk about the Holocaust. Whenever she did so, the therapist began feeling quite anxious. Because of his guilt feelings about the Holocaust, he could scarcely stand to listen to her. As soon as possible he would attempt to change the subject, with the rationale of "stressing the positive."

"What things do you feel positive about in your life right now?" he would ask her.

A cooperative patient, she would dutifully comply by thinking of positive things.

The relationship went on this way for a few months, and the patient became more depressed and would lapse into silence. "I don't know if you're the right therapist for me," she finally said.

"Why's that?"

"I guess because of your German background. I don't think you understand, you know, about the Holocaust."

"Nonsense," he protested. "Of course I understand."

After that session he brought the case to his supervisor and became aware of his guilt feelings, which until that point had been largely unconscious. He went back and confessed those feelings to the patient, and from then on he was able to listen to her about the Holocaust. Both of them grew immeasurably.

Blunder 89

The Jewish Therapist and the WASP Patient

A Jewish therapist had grown up in a cultural atmosphere that prized upward mobility in the WASP world; both his parents spoke with bitterness about how Jews were excluded from that world, and both were determined that their son would make it. However, in attempting to live out that fantasy for his parents, the therapist went through a lot of pain. He was refused admission to a fancy WASP prep school; then, although he was accepted to an Ivy League college, he was pretty much shunned by the WASP majority and lived in a dormitory known as the "Jewish Ghetto." The same situation was repeated in graduate school. He had a great deal of resentment and a general bias towards WASPs by the time he began practicing therapy, some of it quite conscious, some not.

Into his office walked a young man who was the quintessential WASP. He was blond, blue-eyed, tall, and handsome. He came from a very wealthy family and had gone to all the "right" schools. He received a six-figure yearly stipend from a trust fund left by his grandfather. On the surface he had all the smoothness and apparent self-assuredness of a privileged person; however, underneath this veneer was a very insecure, immature little boy.

He had never been able to succeed in his career, nor had he been successful at dabbling in the family financial institution. He was sexually impotent most of the time and had never been able to establish a successful relationship with a woman. What little sexual experience he had was mainly with prostitutes. He was also drinking too much and was afraid he was headed toward being an alcoholic like his father. However, despite all of these problems, he maintained a facade of smugness, superiority, and contempt that covered up his low self-image.

The therapist had an instant negative reaction to his facade and was unable to see the desperate human being beneath; that is, he had an instant cultural counterresistance to analyzing the patient's facade. He reacted to the patient as one of many WASPs who had rejected not only him but also his parents. While listening to the patient describe his negative feelings about himself, the therapist would think, "How can this privileged person have problems? He thinks he has problems? He should hear what I went through." In time, the patient also exhibited a superior, contemptuous attitude toward the therapist (in response to the therapist's silent disapproval of him), which in turn aroused both envy and fury in the therapist. This immobilized him with respect to his being able to confront this behavior as transference and resistance. Unconsciously he wanted the patient to fail, wanted him to end up an alcoholic like his father—and worse. For that reason he was also not inclined to take the risk of confrontation. Hence the therapy went nowhere.

However, the patient's superior attitude became, over a time, quite infuriating to the therapist. He finally discussed the situation with his supervisor, and the supervisor was able to make him aware of his counterresistance. The therapist was then able to get past his stereotyping the patient and to see him as a human being in a lot of pain. After that, he had less trouble penetrating—without rancor—the patient's characterological defense of contempt and superiority and to proceed with analyzing his basic insecurities and their roots in the patient's childhood.

Blunder 90

The WASP Therapist and the Jewish Princess

She was, on the surface, the personification of the JAP (Jewish American Princess). She was an attractive, 39-year-old woman who was convinced she was, if not God's, then perhaps Moses's gift to men. For many years she had worked as a nightclub hostess, in which capacity she had met many men and had exhorted many favors from them; yet none were ever good enough for her. She dressed in expensive yet gauche attire, wore an abundance of jewelry of the most gaudy kind, and had two-inch painted fingernails and a heavily made up face. Her current sessions with her therapist were spent railing at her boyfriend for being too cheap. She complained that the bracelets were not gold enough, that the diamonds in the rings he gave her were not large enough, and the mink coats were not the best brand. She was in a constant state of rage at the man, calling him a "cheap bastard" who did not know how to take care of a woman properly.

The therapist, a woman who was from quite a different heritage, sat during this patient's sessions with her mouth slightly open, thinking to herself, "You've got to be kidding. You're the most outrageous bitch I've ever seen." Naturally, she did not say this, yet it was probably conveyed in her expressions and her body language (she generally sat with folded arms throughout this patient's sessions). The therapist was brought up in a WASP (White Anglo-Saxon Protestant) household in which ostentation and material possessiveness were frowned upon as the greatest possible *faux pas*. Whenever the therapist bought anything for herself, it had to be inexpensive and inconspicuous, and from her own husband she was very careful not to ask for much. In fact, at that moment in time she had just ruled out buying a sports car for herself because it was too showy. She had such a reaction formation against her own greed and exhibitionism–combined with a cultural influence that reinforced that reaction formation–that she was constantly appalled by the JAP patient.

She brought this case to the attention of her supervisor, and he pushed her to deal with her counterresistance to her patient's (and her own suppressed) greed. He helped her to see the patient as an angry, deprived child screaming for attention, admiration, and acknowledgment of her worth. "The demanding, exhibitionistic bitch persona is a defense against her inner pain," the supervisor told her. "Basically, she's a narcissistic personality. The treatment for her involves being a good empathic self-object in order to allow her to experience the acceptance she never received as a child." The therapist heard him and was able to shed her cultural and characterological resistance to the patient's facade and relate to the lonely, needy child inside of her.

Blunder 91

The Italian-American
Therapist and the Puerto Rican Patient

The patient was a beautiful, intelligent, sophisticated 30-year-old Puerto Rican who looked and acted as though she were a white Anglo-Saxon. Although she came into therapy complaining about not being able to relate to men, trouble controlling her weight, and problems with excessive drinking, she maintained at all times a posture of pride and dignity and confidence, as though none of these complaints really mattered. In fact, she had been a successful model, but otherwise her life was empty of any realness. Her narcissistic pride was a defense against the deeper feelings of shame and worthlessness.

Her therapist was a woman who had grown up in an Italian neighborhood in New York in which Puerto Ricans were looked down upon. The therapist had developed a reaction formation against this prejudice and had a strong, unconscious need to prove how unbiased she was towards Puerto Ricans. Although she saw that her patient was excessively proud and knew it was a cover that should be confronted, she was reluctant to do so. She was afraid her patient would think she was biased.

The patient had a resistance to discussing her past or to talking about anything that had to do with her being Puerto Rican, and it was clear that she wanted to forget she was Puerto Rican and forget her past. The therapist colluded with the patient on this; she had a counterresistance to discussing the patient's past or the fact that she was Puerto Rican. Nor did the two ever discuss how the patient felt about being in therapy with an Italian-American therapist.

Because nothing could happen in this therapy situation, the patient slowly eased out of therapy and went to see another therapist who was more at ease with respect to her biases. She quickly moved in to confront the patient's inordinate pride. It turned out that the patient was quite embarrassed and enraged about her background, which was for her a thing of shame and humiliation. Her father was an alcoholic and a womanizer who had been in jail several times; her mother was a high-class call girl. One of her brothers was a heroin addict, and another had been a pusher. As this material emerged, the patient was able to give up her facade – at least in treatment – and get at her deep feelings of shame and humiliation. Her therapy was on its way toward a difficult journey into self-exploration and change.

Blunder 92

The Therapist Who
Did Not Want Her Patient To Be a Housewife

A 23-year-old woman patient had graduated from college but had never pursued a career. She had had a variety of jobs but had never taken any of them seriously. Her stated and avowed aim was to get married, be a housewife, and have children. "I feel so despondent," she told her therapist. "I just wish I could find the right man, a man who wanted marriage and children. It's so hard to find marriage-minded men in the city."

Her therapist was a young woman in her thirties who had a very different attitude about what women should do with their lives. She felt that a woman should be independent and pursue a career. Hence, whenever the patient talked about wanting to find a man, be a housewife, and have children, the therapist was subtly disapproving, and when the patient showed some passing interest in anything that resembled a career, the therapist was encouraging.

The therapist had had a great deal of difficulty getting her own career started and had worked hard to establish independence. Her mother was a dependent woman who had never followed any course outside of the home (like this patient, in effect). The mother became merely an extension of her husband and suffered a loss of self-esteem resulting in a menopausal depression. The therapist was close to her own mother, but she was conflicted between a desire to follow her mother's path and a terror of doing so—fearing to do so would be to lose her identity. So she pushed herself to *not* be dependent on anyone and to establish her independence and her career, at the expense of her personal relationships with men.

The therapy relationship with the woman who wanted to be a housewife aroused not only characterological conflicts in the therapist but also went against the grain of her value system, which was feminist-oriented. Each time the patient spoke of finding the right man, getting married, and becoming a housewife, the therapist would again express disapproval in some form or another. After one such interchange, the patient fell silent, gazing downward in a wan way.

"What's the matter?" the therapist asked.

"Nothing."

"Are you sure?"

"I guess I don't feel accepted by you for who I am and where I want to go."

The therapist brought the case to her supervisor's attention. The supervisor pointed out that the therapist had a counterresistance to the patient's choice of lifestyle. The patient's goal was a threat to the therapist because of her experience with her mother and because of the cultural milieu in which she had grown up, in which independence and a career were valued above being a housewife. Because of this resistance, the therapist had not been able to see that for this patient to be a housewife was not self-negating or masochistic—her own mother had felt *good* about being a housewife and had done quite well at the occupation. This patient looked forward to actualizing her creativity and her humanity by raising a healthy child or two and providing a secure and harmonic home environment for her spouse and children.

When this counterresistance was resolved, the therapist was able to ally herself with the patient's goals, and the focus of therapy shifted to the blocks that were impeding the patient from finding a man who could fulfill her aims. In time she found such a man and was soon leading a satisfying life on her own terms.

Blunder 93

The Masculinist
Therapist and the Ambitious Woman

A bright, attractive, 40-year-old woman went into treatment with the same elderly male therapist who was treating her husband. Whenever she discussed problems she was having with her husband, the therapist invariably took the husband's side. He advised the patient to be the submissive, self-denying, and supportive wife her husband wanted her to be. He discouraged her from pursuing a career. "Your greatest fulfillment," he told her, "should come from keeping your husband happy, your children healthy and happy, and taking care of your home." Her husband was, in fact, a tyrannical, self-centered man; even if being a submissive, self-denying housewife had been this particular patient's goal, she would have received little credit or admiration or love from him. However, these goals were not at all what she wanted out of life. She wanted to be a wife in an egalitarian relationship, and she also wanted a career. She was an intelligent and talented person and wanted to use those capacities to actualize herself as an advertising executive.

This therapist had a resistance to understanding and supporting the patient's feelings and goals with respect to her husband and to her career. His counterresistance was based on an ingrained masculinist value system, with which his core self was identified on a narcissistic, unconscious level. The patient's feelings and goals were contrary to his value system, hence threatening to his self. To accept them meant, unconsciously, the disintegration of his self. He had become identified with this value system through his cultural heritage—he had grown up in a blue-collar neighborhood where patriarchy was the rule—and the system had rigidified over the years. Now he was not able to help his female patient explore her real needs and wishes in an empathic way.

However, with the help of friends, who supported her desire for autonomy, she was able to leave both the therapist and her husband and forge an outstanding career in her field. Ultimately she married a warm, supportive man who admired her ambitiousness and delighted in her independence.

Blunder 94

The Orthodox Analyst
and the Patient Who Wanted To Scream

"I feel like screaming," the patient said.

"What would that do for you?" the therapist asked.

"Release me."

"Release you from what?"

"I don't know. I don't want to talk about it. I just want to do it. But I'm afraid if I did, you'd disapprove of me."

"You feel I'd disapprove of you if you screamed?"

"Yes. You'd think I was being self-indulgent or something."

"What would that mean to you, if you thought I saw you as self-indulgent."

"It would mean, I don't know. I just want to scream. I don't want to talk about it. God, I wish I could just scream."

This dialogue had transpired several times during the course of a month of three-times-a-week analysis. The patient was a young man who had had a torturous upbringing and whose infantile rage had now come to the surface. His therapist was a classically-trained psychoanalyst who had a resistance to screaming. This resistance was both cultural and characterological. Culturally it stemmed from his classical training at a prestigious New York psychoanalytic institute, which emphasized the blank screen, neutrality, abstinence, and a focus on intrapsychic conflicts between the ego, id, and superego. In other words, the approach taught at this institute and practiced by its training analysts, control supervisors, and the like, contained a built-in resistance to emotional ventilation—which was indeed considered self-indulgent and a needless diversion from the primary task of therapy. In addition, this institute still accepted the theory—and it was passed on from generation to generation of therapists—that the Oedipus complex lay at the core of all neuroses; to resolve the Oedipus complex was to obtain a cure. Hence there was a resistance to preoedipal material along with a resistance to emotional ventilation. For this reason, the patient in this case had two strikes against him from the start.

"Sometimes I feel so alone," he would say. "Sometimes I feel so alone I could scream."

"What would that do for you?" the therapist would repeat his standard line.

"I don't know. I don't know what it would do for me. I don't know. I just want to do it. Can't you get that through your head? I just want to do it."

The patient would never be able to scream, not with this therapist. He would have to find another therapist for that, which he did.

Blunder 95

The Therapist Who Believed in Abortion

A patient who was raised in a conservative culture and did not believe in abortion was in therapy with a therapist who had been raised in a liberal culture and had strong feelings in favor of abortion. When the patient became pregnant the subject of abortion was an issue in the therapy.

The patient was a young woman in her early twenties, from a Catholic family. The therapist was a very independent, older Jewish woman. Although the young woman's boyfriend had said he wouldn't marry her, she wanted very much to have the baby anyway, and spoke to the therapist about the pros and cons of having the child.

"I know it would be hard to raise a baby alone, but I just can't see taking a human life," she told the therapist.

"You view getting an abortion as taking a life?"

"Yes I do." The patient was quite adamant. "It *is* taking a life."

"But what about *your* life?" The therapist raised a brow.

"What about it? I'll be okay." The patient sighed and stared at the therapist as though to study her. "I'm starting to feel you don't want me to have the baby. I'm getting the impression you want me to get an abortion. I don't think that's right. I don't think you ought to be doing that. I mean, is that therapeutic?"

At first the therapist denied that she was attempting to influence the patient. "I'm just playing the devil's advocate," she said. However, when she thought about it later, she became uncomfortable.

She discussed it with her supervisor and realized that she did indeed have strong feelings about abortion and was undoubtedly trying to influence the patient. She was imposing her own value system onto the patient, assuming that hers was superior to the patient's. This was causing the patient much distress both because of the therapist's superior attitude (which the patient picked up) and because the therapist's position on abortion went against the grain of the patient's. This patient needed to work things out on her own terms, not on the therapist's terms, and the supervisor pointed this out to the therapist. "If you influence her into getting an abortion when her own superego could not tolerate such a decision, you could end up causing her a lot of mental anguish, which sooner or later would wreak havoc on the therapy relationship," the supervisor told her. The therapist understood.

The therapist acknowledged her resistance to the patient's desire to have her baby and assured her that she would attempt to be more objective from that point on. With the therapist's support, the patient did have the child and became a reasonably good mother.

Blunder 96

The Religious Therapist and the Atheist

When she graduated from college, she entered a school of divinity with the aim of becoming an ordained minister of a Methodist church. However, after a year she became disenchanted with that notion and decided instead to become a therapist, enrolling in a school of social work. She remained a devout Christian throughout her studies, and when she later set up a therapy practice, her conduct was not without a certain missionary zeal.

A patient — a young man whom she had developed a maternal interest for (he would be the son she never had, and whom she would mold in her image) — acknowledged to her one day that he did not believe in God.

"I think religion, like Marx said, is the opiate of the masses."

The therapist was quite offended by this remark, not only because it went against her own beliefs — with which her feelings of self-esteem and self-worth were connected narcissistically — but also because it represented a betrayal of her self object. For these and other reasons she was quite resistant to hearing his opinions on the subject and hastened to cut him off. "But we seem to be getting off the point. The point is that you're having problems with your boss."

"Oh, yes, my boss." The patient complied, went back to discussing his boss, and the topic of religion was dropped; hence an important aspect of the transference and countertransference situation was avoided, "swept under the rug," and the therapy kept from growing, at least in that respect.

However, the therapist now had a new mission—to convert this young man to the "right" way. She was not interested in analyzing the transference (probing why he had made that particular statement at that particular time, how he perceived her, etc.). On the contrary, once he made the statement, her body was flooded with anxiety, as though he had injected a poison inside her. Her only thought was to get the poison out of her system, and his: to exorcise his demons.

In the sessions that followed, whenever she had an opening she would bring up the topic of religion. In a gentle way she attempted to ridicule his atheism and to imply that it was merely a form of acting out against authority, not based on rational thought.

"You'll accept God when you're ready," she would tell him.

Not feeling accepted on his terms, he became even more adamant about his atheism and began ridiculing the therapist's "need for an opiate." He grew more and more disappointed with her as a therapist and, eventually, terminated his therapy sessions with her. "It's not working anymore," he told her.

"I feel extremely saddened by your departure. I truly feel I've failed you. I only hope you find the way on your own. God bless you."

"And Marx bless you," the patient retorted.

Blunder 97

The Conservative Therapist and the Communist

The patient was a man of about middle age who had been brought up in an atmosphere that laid heavy stress on communism as the highest priority in life. His parents had both been officers and active members of the party; they taught the patient to believe that achieving a communist society was possible in America and represented the only opportunity for dealing with the many social and cultural inequities plaguing the country. Although the patient was not actually affiliated with the party, as an adult he still held a communistic view of the world, eschewing the "culture of narcissism" and materialism. His relationships were also colored by the socialistic need to help others who were disadvantaged rather than pursuing his own "selfish" goals.

His therapist, also middle-aged, was politically conservative, and his background was one that put a great deal of emphasis on personal achievement. In the cultural atmosphere in which the therapist grew up, little value was given to matters of the person as a member of a group in the communistic sense. In fact, communists and others in the liberal camp were viewed as bleeding hearts who did not see the world realistically.

When the patient spoke about his relationship to the

community-at-large and the need to espouse social reforms, the therapist tended to deal with such statements by analyzing them as self-effacing defenses against the patient's narcissism and grandiosity.

"If you're *not* a communist when you're 20, you don't have a heart," he once told the patient. "And if you're still a communist when you're 30, you don't have a head."

Although his interpretations about the patient may have been valid, the therapist nevertheless used them to shut the patient up. Because of his resistance to anything that smacked of communism or liberalism, the therapist could not listen empathically to the patient. He could not wait until there was enough trust between the patient and himself so that he could suggest these interpretations in a loving, rather than a subtly hostile, manner. Hence a stalemate developed, and therapeutic progress was stymied for many months.

Blunder 98

The Therapist Who Needed To Prove Her Thesis

Before she had been a therapist she was a college professor, steeped in an academic tradition. Her degree was in social psychology, and she had written her doctoral dissertation on the effects of culture on personality. The dissertation was a study of WASP families. In her view, WASP families were emotional deserts in which feelings were rarely expressed openly. Her thesis focused on the system of punishment and reward in such families, demonstrating how individual expression and emotionality in general were punished and conformity, stoicism, and adaptation rewarded.

A patient came into treatment with her who seemed to be the typical WASP. She was a young woman in her thirties who grew up in Connecticut, whose mother was a Presbyterian and whose father was an Episcopalian. However, her family atmosphere was not typical. Although her father fit into the usual WASP stereotype of the low-key, bland, unemotional man who is removed from wife and children and immersed in his work, his golf, his martinis, and his books, on the other hand, her mother was highly emotional. She ranted and raved, screamed, and was verbally and often physically abusive to the children. The children generally used their mother – who was at least present – as a role model. The patient consequently saw herself as an emotional person.

When the patient attempted to present her childhood as filled with overt emotionalism and conflict, the therapist would frequently counter with statements from her dissertation. "Are you sure your mother was really emotional?" she would ask. "Perhaps, in retrospect, you're blowing things out of proportion."

"No, I'm not blowing things out of proportion."

"Well, all I can tell you is that in my study of 126 WASP families, I never encountered anything like you describe."

"I keep telling you, my family was an exception."

"I suppose so."

The therapist was threatened by this patient's childhood memories of emotionality and physical abuse because it seemed to refute her thesis. Too much of her narcissism was tied up with this thesis and her own academic achievement for her to be able to listen in an unbiased way. Unfortunately, her counterresistance to the patient's past led to a failure to explore the importance of many traumatic situations in her childhood and thereby impeded therapeutic progress and the patient's emotional development.

Blunder 99

The Therapist Who
Wanted To Reform a Call Girl

At a certain point in his career a therapist decided to specialize in reforming prostitutes. He had grown up in a family environment in which women were dominant, including a couple of spinster aunts who frequently spoke vehemently about how women were exploited in American society. Whenever these aunts saw a woman being submissive to a man, they would exclaim, "How can she degrade herself like that?" The young man became imbued with this value system and later, as an adult, he would feel guilty every time he passed a prostitute, thinking to himself, "How can she degrade herself like that?" And so the idea came to him to advertise a special therapy for women "in the life" – as it was called by those in the profession.

One of his first patients was an attractive young woman with bleached blond hair. She told him she had run away from home at 16 and had begun working as a call girl at 17. She was now 21 years old, owned a condominium in Greenwich Village, a sports car, and a house in the country – all of which she had paid off in cash through her work as a call girl. She made $300 an hour, and it would have been impossible for her to earn that kind of money in any other way; to go straight she would have had to make quite a financial sacrifice. At any rate, she had not come to him to change her career, which she did not experience as problematic. She wanted to talk about problems with drugs, with her boyfriend, with her pimp.

"How do you feel about being a call girl?" he would ask her every time the topic of her career came up.

"I feel okay about it. Why do you keep asking me that?"

"Does it ever feel, well, degrading to you?"

"No, not really."

"Never?"

"No. It's a job. What can I tell you?"

"Have you ever thought of modeling?"

"Yeah, I thought about it, but I'm not tall enough and my legs are too thick and my cheek bones are too low. Anyway, it's really hard to get started in that field."

"How about sales? Have you ever thought of going into sales?"

"No, not really. I like being a call girl just fine. It pays the bills. In a few years I'll retire and become a madam, and then after a while I'll make a few million and retire completely. I don't see anything wrong with that, do you?"

The therapist did not answer. Of course he had a different agenda for her, and because of his agenda there was a resistance to understanding the patient on her terms. She was a person who had had an extremely intrusive mother and who was subsequently quite adamant about doing things her way. Her lifestyle was in part an acting out of anger at her mother, who had always warned her that if she did not do as her mother asked, she would end up being a slut. It was as though she were saying now to her mother, "All right, now I am a slut, and I like it fine, so there." The therapist, in attempting to reform her, was replaying the situation with her mother, becoming yet another intrusive person sitting in judgment of her and trying to run her life. In failing to see this and to relate to her on her terms—allowing her to be independent, providing her with a supportive, nonjudging environment until such a time as she herself might wish to begin to address the many real problems inherent in her lifestyle—he only succeeded in alienating her.

Before long she—as well as all the other call girls who responded to his ad—had terminated therapy. Eventually he gave up the idea of specializing in reforming call girls, resumed a regular practice, and went back into supervision.

Blunder 100

The Therapist
Who Would Not Talk on the Phone

"I know you don't like to discuss things on the phone," a female patient said in a pleading voice. "But this is an emergency. It really is."

"I'm sure it is," the therapist, an older woman, replied. "Would you like to set up an appointment for later today?"

"But it's an emergency!"

"I'm sorry, but you know my telephone policy."

"Can't you make an exception just this once?"

"No, I can't."

"Don't you even want to know what the emergency is?"

"Whatever it is, I'm sure it could better be discussed in a regular session."

"Never mind." The patient hung up.

This therapist had decided that any contact with her patients outside the office (including telephone contacts) would becloud the transference and would, furthermore, represent a breakage of the rule of abstinence. In addition, she felt it was important for her to stick to her boundaries, for any fluctuation from the boundaries she had set up might be perceived as a weakness by her patients, which would then encourage attempts at manipulation. These rigidities of technique were rooted in the training she had undergone and in her upbringing, both of which emphasized the strict adherence to rules. At the same time, this patient was one who was constantly challenging the rules, and this was not the first time she had tried to get the therapist to discuss something with her on the telephone. So, in the context of this case, the therapist had additional justification not to bend the rules.

However, she had such a strong resistance towards talking on the phone with this patient that she declined even to hear what the emergency was. That was her mistake, and it was a costly one. For, just this once, the patient actually had a legitimate reason to talk on the phone with the therapist: she had just been raped and was in a state of shock. There are always exceptions to every rule – the therapist knew that – but she was too annoyed at this patient and too rigid to be able to bend. As the result, the patient not only terminated therapy but also sued the therapist for abandonment and won a settlement of several thousand dollars.

Blunder 101

The Therapist Who Would Not Heal Himself

He was a therapist who had trained with most of the top people in the field, taking workshops here and there, but he had a resistance to going into therapy himself. He had come from a long line of physicians and psychiatrists, and nobody in his family had ever needed therapy. Therapy, he felt, was only for sick people. He would be the best, like his father and his grandfather, at helping those sick people.

When he had trained with what he considered were the top therapists in New York, he and his wife moved to a small town and he set up practice.

"I'll have a full practice by the end of the year," he told his wife.

"I'm sure you will, dear," she replied.

Now, as therapists were needed in this town, he succeeded in his aim in only six months. But by two years he had lost all his patients.

"I think I need more training," he told his wife.

"I think so, dear," she replied.

He went to France to study with the top therapists there, in the existential school, then returned to start a practice in another small town.

"This time I'll succeed for sure," he said.

"Yes, dear," his wife said.

Two years later his practice had fallen apart once again.

"I think . . . " he said to his wife.

"You need more training," she finished the sentence.

He went to England to study with the top expert in the object relations school, then returned to set up practice in another small town.

"This time I can't fail," he assured his wife, winking again.

"Of course not, dear," she replied.

Two years later his practice had fallen apart once again.

"I think . . . " he said to his wife.

"You need more training," she finished the sentence.

"You took the words right out of my mouth."

He traveled to far-off places – India, South America, Russia, gathering information on their ways of doing therapy. He came back full of confidence and zeal.

"This is it!" he told his wife. "I've trained with every top therapist in the field, past and present."

"Dear, I was thinking," his wife said. "You trained with all the top therapists, but you haven't been in therapy yourself."

"Why would I need therapy? I'm not sick; they are."

Two years later his practice had once again fallen apart.

The therapist, for the first time, was somewhat sad. He sat in his empty office for a whole day, pondering his fate. His wife came to sit beside him.

"I don't know what to do. I've trained with the top people. I've trained with Rogers and Winnicott and Laing and Fromm. I've trained with the best. I don't understand it." He lapsed into silence.

"You know, dear," his wife replied. "Perhaps you could talk with some of your ex-patients."

The therapist looked at his wife, appalled. "What on earth for?"

"Well, I thought perhaps they could tell you why they left you, and then you might learn something."

"Preposterous," he said, cutting her off. "How could *they* teach *me* anything? What do they know about therapy?"

"Nothing, dear, only," she tried once more, "only, I thought maybe they might, well, be able to tell you something they didn't like about you, something about your personality, say, that put them off, and then . . ."

"That is the most ridiculous thing I've ever heard," he shouted, bolting up. "My personality is fine. How dare you suggest such a thing. How dare you put me down in this way. I don't need a wife who puts me down. I need a wife who supports me. Now I don't want to hear anymore about my personality."

"Yes, dear."

"Actually," he said, feeling a bit better, "now that I think of it, there is one person I still haven't trained with. Yates in Australia. Yes, that's what I'll do. I'll train with Yates for a year. Then I'm sure I will know everything I need to know."

"Of course you will, dear," his wife replied.

"Then I'll come back and set up a practice in the next town."

"I'm sure it will be a wonderful practice," his wife said.

"You bet it will."

A week later he left for Australia.

CHAPTER SEVEN

DIAGNOSIS AND TREATMENT OF COUNTERTRANSFERENCE AND COUNTERRESISTANCE

Richard C. Robertiello, M.D.

A friend of mine had an uncle who, after a stay of many years, was released from a state hospital. Whenever he got into one of his frequent arguments and his sanity was questioned, he would bring out his document of release from the state hospital. "Here," he would say, "is proof that *I* am sane. What proof do *you* have?" Unfortunately, many analysts and other therapists use their completion of a training analysis and their certificate of graduation from an analytic or therapeutic institute in the same manner. They have proof of their mental health, whereas their patients and friends outside the profession have none. They use this illusion about their mental health to deny the existence of their own remaining psychopathology.

This in truth is an illusion that borders on a delusion, that "you don't have to be crazy to be a psychiatrist." Most of the people in our field were motivated toward it by their own anxieties and interpersonal difficulties. We start off with a very skewed sample. The people in our field must admit to having a much greater incidence of psychological problems than, say, dermatologists or dentists or architects (I think I shall omit lawyers from this list). We also know or should know the limitations of our work. There is a phrase in Italian that refers to the chances of change from our efforts: *"Amegliare forse, ma curare mai!"* – "To improve, perhaps; but to cure, never!"

Our chances of reversing our pathology and coming out of our training therapy with a clean bill of health are negligible. Some of this illusion is perpetuated by those analysts who believe that the Oedipus complex is the heart and soul of psychopathology of neurotics. The Oedipus complex can often be resolved; if it indeed is the essence of one's difficulty, then it is not unreasonable that a therapist might feel "cured" by his training analysis. However, now many of us believe that the Oedipus complex is just the tip of the iceberg. If we can be sanguine about the limits of the resolution of the Oedipus complex, we must be equally guarded about more permanent or deep resolutions of all preoedipal material.

We therapists must come forth and acknowledge the existence and persistence of a great deal of psychopathology in ourselves and must drop our defensiveness. We must recognize countertransference and counterresistance as universals – not rare phenomena that only appear in a few aberrant, deviant therapists.

The clearing away of this denial and these illusions about ourselves opens up a new world. The question is no longer, "Do I have countertransferences and counterresistances?" The question becomes, "What kind of countertransferences and counterresistances am I prone to?" This leads to other questions. "How can I categorize them so I will be forewarned and sensitized to certain patients or certain kinds of material? Are they so strong that I should clearly avoid certain patients because I know *a priori* that they will push buttons in me that will be counterproductive to a successful therapeutic outcome? What clues do I have to tell me when a countertransference or counterresistance is rearing its ugly head? What should I do when I discover such a clue?" When I asked the last question of one of my supervisees, he said – jokingly, I trust – "Well, obviously the first thing to do is to completely deny it." I wonder if his jocular answer may be more the case than many of us are willing to admit?

It behooves us to think seriously about the answers to these questions. Let us begin with the first one: "What kind of counter-transferences and counterresistances am I prone to?" To find the answer we look at the parts of our mothers, fathers, and siblings that we did not like or caused us problems. Let me use myself as an example.

I'll start off with an obviously biased and very subjective view of "dear old Mom." My mother was a passive woman who practically did not exist except as an extension of my father. She was constantly depressed and complaining about his abuse of her. She did absolutely nothing with her life and was a constant, subtle guilt-producer to all around her, silently blaming us for her depression. She was not especially intrusive or demanding or controlling. She was in no way a disciplinarian. She was so help-less that she was constantly rejecting me. Since she could not cope with anything, including me, she constantly shipped me off – weekends, vacations, holidays, whenever possible – to relatives. Even in the house she left me to be cared for by maids or grand-parents. What effect does this have on my countertransferences and counterresistances? Well, on the positive side, I am much less negatively reactive than most of my colleagues to "Jewish mothers." I cannot only tolerate but almost welcome women who are intrusive or controlling. I like "care packages" and chicken soup. I can deal with some female patients easily while those same females drive some of my colleagues to destruction. On the negative side, I am overly sensitive to rejection by female patients. I tend to have contempt for women who do not actualize themselves. One of my colleagues put it critically, saying that I "grew balls on women." In fact, I am very admiring and sup-portive of women's career efforts. This has been a plus for many of my patients. One very big negative is that I am extremely re-active in an angry way to women who "run guilt trips" on men and on me. Patients who are never able to be satisfied or made happy represent a failure of my infantile omnipotent wish to change my mother. The same is true of my reactions to women who accuse me of failing them or who are "professional victims" or who accuse men of being the reason their lives are ruined. Obviously I am being schematic. I know that my mother was more and perhaps also less than the way I have described her. And I know that my countertransferences to women encompass a great many more nuances than what I have described. But what I *have* said is true. I have in my internal computer the knowledge that these kinds of women and these kinds of issues tick me off and make me prone to irrational reactions.

Now let's take "dear old Dad." He for me was a two-headed monster, in more ways than one. I had a split father-figure–my real father and my father's father–my paternal grandfather. Both of them lived in the same house with me throughout my childhood. They were quite different. My father was a very busy physician who thankfully was rarely in the house during my waking hours. When he came home, I would often hide in the bathroom. He was angry, ferocious, menacing, and incredibly competitive with me for my mother's attention. His father, my grandfather, was also frightening; he was a cruel, harsh disciplinarian who terrorized me with a strap he did not hesitate to use. He was intent on making me his narcissistic extension and required "all work and no play" from me as well as constant perfection. So with this happy childhood experience with men, I have to know that I am very negatively reactive to men who are either competitive or else controlling and authoritarian. This awareness hopefully helps me avoid certain pitfalls. At least I do not approach men like these blindly; and when a patient has any of these qualities, I am usually alert to countertransference feelings about them.

My most important sibling was a beloved but also hated sister, who died when she was 5 and I was 7. I felt tremendous guilt over her death since she upstaged me. Yet she was the only member of my household for whom I felt love and from whom I received affection. When I see a particularly vulnerable young lady, I am likely to have a too strongly positive and at times erotic countertransference. I may also have more than a normal stake in bringing a wounded bird back to life; this is to expiate my guilt and also to prove once again my infantile omnipotence. In this case a knowledge of my propensities will hopefully keep me from falling too deeply into countertransference reactions or at least help me to deal with them more swiftly, before they have done any major harm.

I have used myself as an example because I would like to be a model to other therapists with respect to being open to themselves and also to their peers, colleagues, and supervisors about their psychopathology. After the first year or two, supervision should deal mainly with the therapist's countertransferences and counterresistances. By then most of the errors will not be caused by lack of knowledge or by mistakes in technique.

What, then, are the clues that may tell us when we are caught up in a countertransference or counterresistance reaction? These become obvious once we acknowledge them. One such clue is a feeling of distaste about a patient's expected appearance. Others include making a mistake in scheduling, such as putting two patients in the same hour or forgetting an appointment with a patient. At times we may forget a patient's name, or we may notice that we become anxious during a patient's session. We may find our mind wandering during a session or that we are drowsy. Having a dream about a patient is a clue that should not be ignored. The same is true for fantasies—erotic, competitive, hostile, or even rather banal—about a patient. Dreams and fantasies always, in my opinion, have their roots in childhood experience. The presence of a patient in either a dream or fantasy is a signal that the patient represents some figure from our past. Slips of the tongue made during a session should alert us that something may be amiss, as should other slips, ending the session before the allotted time or prolonging a session, being repeatedly late for a patient or starting a patient's sessions early. Allowing a patient to incur a big debt is often motivated by more than altruism, though it may also under certain circumstances be appropriate. The same can be said of giving a patient a great deal of extra time on the phone outside the treatment hour. Socializing with a patient outside the office, while it may not always be detrimental or inappropriate, always needs scrutiny. As a general rule, we tend to follow a routine in our dealings with most of our patients. If our behavior with a particular patient is quite different, we should wonder what may be prompting a departure. Mistakes in billing should not be overlooked as simply an error in arithmetic. Over all, we should be the constant objects of our own observation, looking for any intense feelings about patients, and being vigilant about what the next instant will be in which our unconscious mind may betray us.

An unanalyzed, briefly analyzed, or poorly analyzed therapist does not have a prayer. We have become more aware of the difficulties Freud had with his patients, despite his brilliance. This is also true of those recipients of brief analyses from Freud and others at the beginning of the century who had major difficulties with their patients. Doing therapy without the benefit of an extensive and deep analysis is comparable to doing surgery with a dull spoon. Freud himself recommended that analysts go back for analysis every five years. I heartily concur. Since there is no "cure," the problems are apt to present themselves in different forms at different stages in the life cycle. And also some problems that were not visible at one point may rear their ugly heads later on. An example might be the difficulty in dealing with our mortality, a difficulty that can increase with age. Long, deep, and repeated analyses—preferably with different analysts of both sexes—is one way of keeping open the pathway from the unconscious to the conscious; this will certainly be extremely helpful in avoiding or quickly picking up countertransferences and counterresistances. And it will also help dispel the delusion that one is "fully analyzed" and has no barrier between his conscious and unconscious. Breaking through repression and other defenses should be a process that goes on continually in an analyst's life.

We have had the proper analytic preparation and have thought about what kinds of patients or situations can touch off irrational reactions in us. We have also been vigilant in observing ourselves. We have picked up one or more of the clues – for example, a patient has appeared in one of our dreams. Now comes the first and hardest test. Shall we – as my supervisee answered when asked what he does when he becomes aware of a clue – completely deny it? That is unfortunately what many of us will do. In this instance we must come to grips with the situation and make the sometimes dreaded diagnosis of countertransference or counterresistance or both! We must acknowledge this is occurring in working with patients. That is more than half the battle. But it is not the end of the battle. Making the diagnosis is necessary, but not nearly sufficient. What do we do next? After the diagnosis comes the treatment.

If we are experienced and have had personal psychoanalysis, supervision, peer counselling, etc., we may be able to work through our resistance and get to see who or what the patient represents to us that causes us to mix him or her up with some past figure or some past or even present issue in our lives. If we are fortunate and open enough to our own unconscious process, we may see an electric light bulb, the third eye of enlightenment, ablaze across our minds. We may then be clear what our reaction was about and able to transcend it without further help from outside sources. This can happen, especially with experienced analysts, who have experienced innumerable such reactions throughout the years and have an insight into their own foibles. If there is a persistence of any of the clues, they hopefully will know that they have not succeeded on their own and need outside assistance.

For an inexperienced therapist there should be an expectation of multiple problems in countertransference and counterresistance. The new therapist needs interminable analyses but also ongoing, deep supervision – which includes using process notes and perhaps a tape recorder or a two-way mirror or a video recorder. Only through this kind of arduous and exacting process can a young analyst begin to understand the pattern of his irrationalities. Hopefully even after a formal length of time in supervision–preferably with more than one supervisor, because supervisors have their blind spots too–the beginning analyst might return to supervision when confronted with indications of countertransference difficulties and, unable to understand their occurrence, cannot resolve them.

I remember the moment in my practice when I realized that I had no longer the need of supervision. It was at first more frightening than exhilarating. When a therapist has achieved this status and begins to get clues of a countertransference or a counterresistance, he naturally will try to decipher it on his own and be successful. If this is not possible, it becomes necessary to discuss the situation with a colleague. At this level a supervisor seems inappropriate, but a discussion with a peer is mandatory.

When I first began doing therapy I expected to have countertransference reactions to almost all of my patients. I was unfortunately not disappointed in this prediction. In the middle years of practice–between the tenth and twentieth years–I expected and allowed myself three or four *serious* countertransferences or counterresistances a year. Usually, however, I did not have that many. I felt this represented par for the course at that stage in my development. And when I use the word "serious," I mean a countertransference that disturbs me or has the potential of being disruptive to the therapeutic process. Minor countertransferences or counterresistances occur daily, even to the most experienced therapist. But they are quickly diagnosed and disposed of without outside help and do not have a large impact on the course of therapy. After twenty years or so, the incidence of *serious* irrational reactions tends to be rare. (One reason for this is that an experienced therapist can often select his patients. With this privilege, one can avoid the kinds of patients one knows from experience have a greater possibility of provoking countertransference reactions.) The minor countertransferences do persist, even after twenty years of clinical experience, and still need constant attention to prevent them from becoming serious.

Many of my colleagues—even those with many years of experience—continue self-scrutiny in peer groups. This admission of vulnerability and acknowledgment of the necessity for objective feedback is laudable. It represents one way of dealing with the ubiquitous nature of these phenomena and the constant potential of their subtle intrusion into our treatment efforts. A supervision or peer group can often have greater impact than an individual supervisor or peer.

When a patient comes into treatment, we are confronted with an awesome responsibility. A psychotherapist can help bring about a life of psychotic suffering or one of relative tranquility. We have an awesome responsibility because of our power. Patients generally regress in treatment, often to a state of helplessness and extreme vulnerability. This regression is often necessary and helpful to the therapeutic outcome. But it also puts the patient in a position in which any mishandling by the therapist can do damage. We have included a few cases in which therapists consciously or unconsciously exploited patients for their own sexual, emotional, or financial gain. I have described these situations and labeled them as cases of iatrogenic psychiatric illness—illnesses caused by therapists. The patient's susceptibility is heightened by the need to unite with a beneficent parental figure. Being exploited by an unscrupulous therapist can bring out a loss of ego boundaries, serious identity confusion, and often major consequences in the patient's relationships or career. Now, fortunately, these situations are relatively rare in our profession; but just as we can learn about the "normal" from the "abnormal," we can learn about the effects of countertransference and counterresistance by studying these extreme examples. These extreme situations damage a patient more than do those involving more normal, unconscious kinds of countertransference and counterresistance. In the latter, the damage may be more in terms of *what might have occurred* but was thwarted. Nevertheless, there has been too little attention in our field to this issue of therapists damaging their patients.

This book brings the issues surrounding countertransference and counterresistance to light through clinical situations—situations with which every therapist is all too familiar. The cases we presented represent, in the main, actual clinical situations—from our own experiences or those of colleagues. It is important to be able to look at these occurrences without guilt. They do not occur because we lack integrity or are extraordinarily neurotic. They are universal. They occur because we are all human and fallible. We are dealing with delicate instruments—our patients' psyches and our own. We cannot expect our own to be so finely tuned that they will not be askew at times. Countertransferences and counterresistances are part of our professional experience. Leaving aside the induced countertransferences and counterresistances that are helpful in our treatment, the ones that come mainly from our own irrationalities can never be totally eliminated and must be continually confronted, acknowledged, and dealt with effectively. The only irresponsible act is not admitting to countertransference and counterresistance, denying their existence and posturing as paragons of mental health.

Confronting and resolving our countertransferences and counterresistances can reduce their negative impact to a tolerable minimum. It is our way of healing ourselves so we can heal our patients.